THE SWEDEN FILE

THE SWEDEN FILE

Memoir of an American Expatriate

Second Edition

Letters and Comments by

Bruce Stevens Proctor, 1943-2011

Compiled and Edited,

with Reflections by

Alan Robert Proctor

Open Books Press
Bloomington, Indiana

ADVANCE REVIEW COPY
Not for retail sale
Publication Date: September 3, 2019
Contact info@openbookspress.com with questions or reviews

Published by Open Books Press, USA

www.OpenBooksPress.com
info@OpenBooksPress.com

An imprint of Pen & Publish, Inc.
www.PenandPublish.com
Bloomington, Indiana
(314) 827-6567

Paperback ISBN: 978-1-941799-69-7
e-book ISBN: 978-1-941799-70-3

Library of Congress Control Number: 2019940243

Printed on acid-free paper.

Praise for
The Sweden File:
Memoir of an American Expatriate

"A conscientious objector flees enlistment in Vietnam by making a new life in Sweden . . . . Bruce Proctor's memoir, compiled and edited by his younger brother, poet and novelist Alan Robert Proctor (*Adirondack Summer, 1969*), revisits the late 1960s: the horrors of total war in Vietnam, the unpredictable tides of the American counterculture, and the feeling of being young in a mad world. "Not fear of death, but fear of not being able to live while taking part in killing" is what drives Bruce to renounce his citizenship and leave the country when the National Guard is called up in 1968 . . . . Editor Proctor has obviously put great patience and care into selecting these fragments and the time was well-spent: readers are never bored, always engaged, and often charmed by the liveliness of Bruce's prose (and Alan's poetry scattered throughout the text) . . . . Neither brother holds his tongue in this collection, and readers are richer for it."

—*Kirkus Reviews*

Chosen as a "best read" for 2015, one of only 12 memoirs selected nationally.

December 11, 2015, *The Kansas City Star*

". . . unblinking truth . . . It's rare . . . no grandstanding . . . self acclamation here, only human beings striving to undo the sorrow of war the best they can . . . [and] understand [this] aspect of American history neglected and subverted by politicos . . . . No, in some beautiful way [*The Sweden File*] is a celebration of the heart's love of life and truth. Bravo!"

—Jimmy Santiago Baca, author,
winner of an American Book Award for Poetry,
recipient of the Hispanic Heritage Award for Literature

". . . This book, with its counterpointed perspectives, intimate epistolary narratives, and later commentary, bridges distances of time and place, bringing into focus years when few were spared the grief and sacrifices of a nation led into a distant war that should never have been born . . . ."

—**David Ray**, poet essayist and memorist and winner of the Allen Ginsberg Poetry Award and the William Carlos Williams Award

"Most of us will never find ourselves in a situation in which doing what's morally right is a serious threat to our well-being. [In] *The Sweden File*, [Bruce Proctor] . . . faced such a situation and made the life-rending choice. It's an account of a quiet, sustained heroism."

—**William Trowbridge**, Missouri Poet Laureate from 2012–2016 and Distinguished University Professor Emeritus at Northwestern Missouri State University

Also by Alan Robert Proctor

Adirondack Summer, 1969 – a novel

"I could never have done it. I would never have thought to try, which is even worse."

—Lt. Daniel [Dan] H. Proctor, USNR, after hearing of his brother's desertion from his activated National Guard Unit.

Bruce Proctor's Dedication
and Acknowledgments

To all who supported me and my wife, Rosemary, in times of need: my family in the United States, Bert, Vesna, and many others in Sweden and Canada, including Jimmy Carter, Sven Erlander, and Pierre Trudeau.

The Swedish letters and memories would not have come to be if my brother Alan hadn't compiled the letters and given me a framework on which to reminisce. The letters date from July 1968 to the summer of 1972. My memories are from 40 years later: 2008 and 2009. Alan's reflections and comments are scattered throughout the text.

Alan Robert Proctor's
Acknowledgments

To Bob Stewart for aid in promoting the memoir; to Catherine Browder for helpful comments; to Mary-Lane Kamberg, Dawn Downey, and Deborah Shouse, facilitatiors, and to their members of the Kansas City Writer's Group; to Denise Low for alerting *The Kansas City Star* about the book; to Jo McDougall for help with the memoir genre; to Westphalia Press for an initial printing of *The Sweden File*, and finally to my brother, Daniel Proctor, my sister Carol Kozlevcar, and my wife, Susan Proctor, for never losing faith in the project.

Contents

Praise for *The Sweden File*   5

Preface by David Ray   13

Introduction   16

CHAPTER ONE

AWOL   20

CHAPTER TWO

Our Roots Are in the Sky   44

CHAPTER THREE

Winterfunk   74

CHAPTER FOUR

Notes on the Revolution   84

CHAPTER FIVE

Knife at My Throat   96

CHAPTER SIX

Blue Collar Immigrant   106

CHAPTER SEVEN

Taxi Driver   124

CHAPTER EIGHT

Kayak Trip and Other Pleasant Dangers   142

CHAPTER NINE

Yoga, Booze, and Dope   164

CHAPTER TEN

Canadian Road Trip   182

CHAPTER ELEVEN

"I Must Get Out of Here"   198

CHAPTER TWELVE

Status: Landed   206

Preface by David Ray

Bruce Proctor's ethical dilemma about participating in the Vietnam war was fired not only by the guilt of having served in the secret conduct of war until he could stomach no more, but also by a profound leading to follow his conscience rather than giving into the pressures that lead men to sacrifice their lives. It is a misfortune for a man to give his life for a cause he has been persuaded to believe, but it is a tragedy when a man gives his life for a cause he knows to be wrong.

Regardless of how punitively stigmatized for disobeying state power, one who makes a stand against war must engage courage as weighty as that summoned by warriors in any cause. We do not need to march with Gandhi or Martin Luther King Jr. to understand what is at stake when we confront authority or disagree with Thomas Hobbes and Machiavelli that we must serve right up to the abyss of death at a king's or tyrant's whim. The dice are loaded both against the killers and their victims.

Bruce Proctor refused to be a part of the evil. When my 19-year-old son, Samuel, was killed in an accident, that reality was the only solace I could find—that he would never be part of the evil. Young men find it very hard to resist the allure of brave adventures, and I am not sure Sam could have resisted the false promises of recruiters who stalk high school corridors.

Bruce Proctor clearly saw that his country was mired in a conflict as needless and futile as the Peloponnesian wars Thucydides recorded for posterity with the obvious hope that he would awaken those who have no memories of the horrors. But for every wise man, there are many charismatic enthusiasts for war. Those of a fresh generation can rarely resist.

"I wake each morning and wonder who our masters are today," Bruce wrote, "but somehow they never seem to change; or are always changing but acting the same anyway." After having that insight, a man—or woman—has two choices, to give in to the pressure to serve despite being well aware that the cause is evil, or to refuse.

In the Vietnam War Canada and Sweden were among the few havens offering protection from grim punishment of jails and hefty fines. As my university students were recruited as cannon fodder in the 1960s, with little if any respect for their freedom of thought and action, a huge percentage violated their consciences by obeying even as their doubts grew, were reaffirmed, and ever escalating, even as they were drawn into combat. Grieving widows, some of my students among them, mourned not only their lost loved ones, but the tragedy resulting from the costliest of mistakes. It had long been clear that the war was misguided, deceit-driven, and doomed to defeat.

In Alan Proctor's poem, "Lure" (included in the text of this book), there is a haunting line, which I interpret as expressing the profound ambivalence one feels when contemplating the risks and responsibilities of action in hazardous waters. "How can we explain the pride our lives require?" (Wouldn't it take a book?) It is hard to disentangle the pride of holding firm to an unconditional ethical imperative, such as the Commandment not to kill, an injunction that even in Christian nations is "more honored in the breach than in the observance." The poem ends this way:

> A cold morning:
> my next-door neighbor died in the war,
> my brother deserted; I fish like a crazed sea dog
> until the sun disappears, clouds slice their wrists . . .
> Forgive us fish . . .

How can we explain the pride our lives require?

Alan Robert Proctor, *New Letters*

I have, both in the Vietnam and Iraq wars, heard preachers ranting from the pulpit in praise of "patriotism." e.e. cummings, who had his own problems with World War I, wrote a poem praising a man who refused to take up arms, comparing a C.O.'s extreme punishment with Christ's crucifixion:

i sing of Olaf glad and big
whose warmest heart recoiled at war:
a conscientious object-or . . .
unless statistics lie he was
more brave than me: more blond than you.

"You'll never have a quiet world till you knock the patriotism out of the human race," wrote George Bernard Shaw in 1915. And in January of 1861, the Civil War's sacrifices locked into a certainty, Thomas Corwin wrote in a letter from Washington, DC, that "Treason is in the air around us everywhere. It goes by the name of patriotism."

This book, with its counterpointed perspectives, intimate epistolary narratives, and later commentary, bridges distances of time and place, bringing into focus years when few were spared the grief and sacrifices of a nation led into a distant war that should never have been born. It is particularly provocative and poignant that these exchanges are rich not only with illumination of ethical and other issues, but with the radiance of a loving family unwilling to let their closeness be compromised by any distance or challenge.

Introduction

"Did I ever tell you I was going to be secretary of state someday?"

—Bruce S. Proctor, September 1962

In 1968, my brother Bruce Proctor deserted his Air National Guard unit and fled to Sweden to seek humanitarian asylum. Prior to his employment with the Guard, he worked in the Pentagon for the Defense Intelligence Agency (DIA) as an aerial photographic interpreter. He was responsible for assessing photos taken by the US Air Force fighters flying reconnaissance over Vietnam.

He suddenly quit the agency when he enlarged some of the images and realized that US war planes were murdering Vietnamese civilians. To this day I think of Michelangelo Antonioni's 1966 film *Blow-Up* and the photographer-protagonist's realization, after enlarging a photo he casually took in a park, that the grainy image in the background reveals a dead woman and the gunman nearby. The crime, however, is never brought to light. Bruce wrote about his own troubling discovery of a bombed village not on the designated bomb target: "Well, if the damage doesn't get reported," he notes with Orwellian logic, "then it must not exist . . ."

Bruce's decision to leave the DIA created serious concern in the Pentagon; he had top secret clearance. On advice from friends, he joined the Air National Guard to avoid conscription and, possibly, the long arms of the Federal Bureau of Investigation (FBI) and Central Intelligence Agency (CIA). When his unit was nationalized by President Lyndon Johnson and ordered to Vietnam, Bruce felt he had no choice but to leave the country of his birth.

In 1973 when I began to collect Bruce's letters written during his Swedish exile (1968–1972), I was 25 years old—my brother's age when he deserted. At the time, I was unsure of my motives for the project. Perhaps it was because I was a fledgling writer and poet, one who admired the elements of compelling prose and poetry. My brother was a gifted, if somewhat quirky, writer. He could be humorous, pragmatic, philosophical, obtuse, and mystical all in one paragraph. Perhaps a younger brother's veneration toward his older sibling for taking such a drastic and, to my mind, courageous step played a part.

I thought Bruce captured the freewheeling nature of the late 60s and early 70s with unique perspective: that of an American exile. Whatever the reason for my obsession with the correspondence, I spent months collecting letters to and from him during his time in Sweden. Then, I got on with my life—I fell in love, married, moved, and started working. The letters yellowed with age and remained in a file for 35 years.

When I retired from work, writing—an endeavor I had pursued part-time my entire life—occupied most of my waking hours. Rummaging in a file, I discovered an unfinished novel along with some poetry and prose. But the letters seemed to rustle in the filing cabinet. "Look at us again," they beckoned. So, I pulled them back into the light and transcribed them from the original Royal typewriter manuscript to a digital word document. I sent the entire manuscript to my brother and suggested that he reminisce on his youthful correspondence. I wanted to know what was really going on between some of the gleefully idealistic lines. What were the circumstances of his poverty and despair implied in some of the later letters? He took my suggestion to heart and recounted a more complete panorama of his banishment.

As I read through his later comments, I realized I could expand the discourse by interspersing them among the earlier letters. This would provide some personal and historical context. Our family has its share of writers and historians. Our great-grandfather kept a diary during his service as an enlisted soldier in the Civil War. The diary now resides in the Beineke Rare Book Library at Yale University. My father, Bob, an amateur historian and avid genealogist, brought our family's history to life with old photos and charts detailing ancestral bloodlines. Bob kept a journal his entire life and only abandoned it in his late 80s when dementia set in. Perhaps I could continue the literary and historical tradition with *The Sweden File: Memoir of an American Expatriate.*

Whatever the reason for starting the project, the result was a hybrid—a dual memoir and a collection of historical correspondence. *The Sweden File*'s narrative voice shifts back and forth between letters to and from Bruce, his reminiscences 40 years later in 2008 and 2009, and my reflections in 2014 on the interplay of our shared experience. Headings for each of the three voices identify the perspectives: the LETTERS; Bruce, 2008/2009; and Alan, 2014.

Bruce died from a never-diagnosed disease with unflinching grace in 2011. After nearly 10 agonizing and unfruitful months in hospital, he demanded to be released knowing his final days at home would be very few. And they were: less than a week. It was his final act of courage.

Alan Robert Proctor,
Kansas City, MO, 2014

Chapter One
AWOL

LETTERS

Saturday, July 13, 1968
(posted in New York City)

Dear Folks,

There was reason, after all, for resignation to my fate. If I had really planned to go I would have been very morbid. I have no desire to assist in the death of people. The war in Vietnam is irrational, immoral and stupid. I'm on the bus to New York where I'll fly to Stockholm, Sweden tonight. Rosemary[1] will follow in 3-4 weeks after liquidating our modest property. I'll write as soon as I have an address in Stockholm. We know people there, so I'll be staying with friends. My first problem will be the language, but the government has free courses. There will be no problem with working; the Swedish law is very liberal with political refugees; they enjoy a sanctuary. Naturally, I do not plan to return unless there is, eventually, a legal way to do it. The Swedes run a rational social order so there will be no problem with ordinary amenities of health and living. My strength and certainty that this is the right decision grows; I can feel that it is right. I do not seek an escape or transformation, I'm merely changing my territorial basis. Thanks for a wonderful visit. Now you see why we wanted to take off with *all* the

---

1   Bruce's wife

presents. Don't worry, Mom, I'm never going to volunteer for anything again.

The military authorities will probably be in contact with you by Wednesday or Thursday since I'll be AWOL as of midnight, Tuesday (July 16th). I left your address as the forwarding address and the destination of my leave. They don't have any business with Rosemary, so don't tell them where she is (she'll be staying with Mark[2] until the middle of next week and after in Cranbury, New Jersey). I'm hoping they forward my paycheck for the 15th. If so, please forward to Rosemary. They've been underpaying me anyway! Come and see us when you take your European tour upon retiring.

Love always from your devoted son, Bruce

Bruce, 2008–2009

My "folks" were my mother, Ella Mae, and my father, Bob. I was born at Vallejo Naval Air Station, on San Francisco Bay, June 30, 1943. The first thing that Ella Mae remembers the delivering doctor saying was, "My God, what a head." As it turned out, I was normal, but my head was huge. I did not meet my father until I was six months old and cried upon being presented to the stranger. Bob was in the navy and had been away in the Pacific flying PBYs[3], transporting senior officers and priority cargo, such as battle maps.

In July 1968, I had just turned 25, had been married to Rosemary for seven months, and had received orders to go to Vietnam. I was fleeing the Unites States, booked on a Scandinavian Airlines System flight to Stockholm, leaving Kennedy International. On the bus from Washington, DC, to New York, I sat in the front. I was not taking any chances on not getting there and wanted to talk to the driver if necessary.

"Been to New York often?" I asked.

"My first trip," the driver responded.

"Oh?"

---

2   A friend who sublet Bruce and Rosemary's apartment when they went to Sweden

3   Amphibious planes

As we approached New York through the bottomlands of New Jersey, a route well known from innumerable trips from Washington, DC to East Hampton on Long Island in my youth, the driver was pulling into the lane that would exit to the Holland Tunnel. "Not this exit," I said, "the Holland Tunnel will take you way downtown. You want the Lincoln Tunnel, which gets you to the bus terminal between 40th and 42nd Street."

"Are you sure?" asked the bus driver.

"Very sure—trust me."

"OK then; thank you. This is a big city, isn't it?"

Stowing my bag in a coin key locker at the bus depot, I went out to the curb, hailed a taxi to an address in the upper east 90s. I was passed-in by the doorman and took the elevator.

I found the apartment number and rang the bell. I sensed being scrutinized through the peephole.

"Who is it?" a voice from within asked.

"It's Bruce." The door unlocked, and a middle-aged woman let me in. "I was told that a key might be available for a place in Stockholm," I said, not knowing if this were a setup or not, but trusting the security of my network and not seeing the sense in any delay or evasion—I had only hours to catch the flight to Stockholm.

"Oh, yes," she said, "I heard . . . I have been waiting for you . . . such an undertaking!" I studied her—an attractive woman in her 40s or 50s, agitated and alone.

With the key and the Stockholm address securely in my pocket, I took a cab back to the bus station, retrieved my bags, and found the bus to Kennedy International. Having checked in without a problem, I took my boarding pass, posted the [July 13th] letter to my folks, and found a place to sit and wait in the terminal.

I had brought a book to read but could not concentrate on it. I had dressed casually so as not to attract attention and I cursed the military haircut that might give me away. I had to remind myself not to succumb to the paranoia creeping into my spine, the animal instinct to crouch, look closely at people wandering in the aisles, some of them looking for someone, wondering if *that* guy was going to approach me, ask for ID, and arrest me.

The wait seemed interminable, but I eventually boarded and found my window seat on the left side of the big jet. Taking off over

Long Island, heading east, I gazed down at the Atlantic beaches. Soon, however, clouds obscured the view and I was not able to spot the South Fork, East Hampton, or Three Mile Harbor. I cried. It came over me suddenly, no tears at first, just a shuddering in my chest and an effort to breathe normally. Never again to play in the surf, sit in the dunes, share lunch on the beach, go skin-diving and fishing in the harbor. Never again to take out the kayak, paddle in the early-morning fog. All these memories washed through me in long sobs. And, just to compound all that, thoughts of others followed in quick succession: the loss and unknown reaction of my mother, father, brothers, and sister.

On the long flight to Oslo and Stockholm, I gazed at the Greenland icecaps, an eerie dome of luminescence in the midnight sun, slightly below the horizon, spreading a rose hue from below.

Alan, 2014

Secretary of State John Foster Dulles was largely responsible for anti-American feelings in many developing nations when I was growing up as Bruce's younger brother in the 1950s. John Foster Dulles's brother Allen Dulles was the CIA director during his brother's term as secretary of state. Together, they minted an American corporate colonialism that still lingers today. In 1962, when I was 14 and my brother was in college, Bruce wrote to me and boasted that he would be secretary of state someday.

I can't blame the Vietnam conflict solely on the Dulles brothers, but they endorsed with all their political powers events that eventually sucked the United States into the war, and it was because of this war that my brother felt he had to leave the country of his birth. Bruce, a young American just graduated from college with a degree in international relations, was considered intellectual talent and pursued by both the Central Intelligence Agency (CIA) and the Defense Intelligence Agency (DIA). He chose the DIA.

LETTERS

Monday, 15 July
Stockholm

Dear Folks,

I arrived in Stockholm Sunday morning after an eight-hour flight. Enjoyed seeing the Lake region from Maine to Labrador. Local early morning time, I saw the Orkney Islands and the Norwegian mountains. Landed in Oslo and then here. A friend of Rosemary's, Bert, picked me up at the airport and took me to Lillemor Erlander's house. I had gotten the key from her mother in New York. Sunday, I slept, and Bert picked me up in the evening. We ate downtown and walked around. What a beautiful city! Many canals, old buildings, narrow streets; a very busy, efficient, free, and rational society. They were annoyed by people writing on the buildings, so they built a park with special walls to write on and wooden soap-boxes to speak from. The landscape is glacial rock, clean air with poplars, pines, and birch. The summer here is great. Temperatures around 60°F. I have yet to register with the police and am seeing people today about it. Everyone has been wonderful to me. Luckily, because of Rosemary, I have several very helpful contacts. No sense in telling the M. P.s where I am. I'm playing it cool here and not getting involved in any publicity, groups, or political activity. I hope to get a job before three months are out. By that time Rosemary and I should be settled. Do not worry; life here is better than imperial warfare. So far, the adjustment has been very easy. I haven't had a qualm yet, only joy and astonishment at the rule of reason in this Nordic country. I will be writing Alan, Dan, and several other friends. You will probably have talked with Rosemary by the time you get this. I miss her already and hope she has no problem getting things settled. No problems with money.

My love, Bruce

Bruce, 2008–2009

Rosemary had met Bert and Lillemore when she was in Stockholm during her junior year abroad. I had an older brother, Dan, an older sister, Carol, and a younger brother, Alan. Father Bob would brag, "Oh yes, Alan, Bruce, Carol, and Dan . . . ABCD," as if he had planned it, in reverse chronological order.

With a big smile, Bert found me easily at *Arlanda* airport and we headed to the parking lot where Bert had left his Volvo. I sized up Bert. He was 6'3" or more, taller than me and older, starting to bald with mostly gray hair, but a lively step and an energetic attitude. I touched the key in my pocket and was told that the safe house was in a southern suburb of Stockholm . . . that the airport was north of the city.

As we went through the center of the city, Bert pointed out that only days before, all of Sweden had switched to driving on the right-hand-side of the road, that the arrangements of many intersections were new to him . . . He was glad that this was a Sunday morning and the traffic was very light.

Bert did not accompany me to the door of the safe house but waited until he saw that I had gained entry, then waved through his open window and left.

I wandered through the deserted two-story, side-by-side, noticing the lever-action door passages, the strange design of the light switches, the compact design, the clean lines of the furniture, the different design of the bathroom and kitchen fixtures, the small lot, the big windows and the blinds I would soon learn that kept the bedroom dim during the day, and through the twilight of the night outside, which never got dark. Pulling the blinds, tired from the long trip, I fell into bed. Later that same Sunday afternoon, Bert called to invite me to dinner.

"I'll pick you up in half an hour," he said.

Driving to the Old Town, over unfamiliar roads to a narrow street just below the west side of the royal castle, Bert noted, "Here we are." Once seated and the menus proffered, Bert said, "Whatever you want."

The food arrived, and I was hungry after the trip and the day's sleep. With the meal over and some wine left in the bottle, Bert asked, "So . . . have you thought about the implications of your decision?"

"How so?" I asked.

"The consequences; have you thought you made a mistake and might go back?"

I didn't think I had made a mistake and had no thoughts of going back and said so, tentatively, for this was an important question, one that Bert had wanted to ask and had waited until this moment to do so.

I pondered this further, especially "the consequences." I remembered the flight from New York to Stockholm, even the light blue trim on the tennis shoes of one of the baggage handlers at the stop in Oslo, seen from the window of the plane, on the ground in Scandinavia, far from home. No, I did not want to go back. Something to do with fate and the casting of the die, with too many bridges burned and no way to rationalize a retreat.

But the consequences, yes, that was the rub. I reviewed them in my mind: a warrant out for my arrest in the United States, and possibly to be disowned by my family and never to see them again. As far as I knew, none of my family knew where I was, except that I had received orders to go to the *Tan Son Hout* airbase outside of Saigon. "Consequences, yes; I don't think I'll go back."

Bert mentioned that it was probably time to visit the police and apply for landed immigrant status on humanitarian grounds. He explained that other US servicemen had arrived, and the government had made provision to accept them on these grounds. This was linked to Swedish neutrality regarding the Vietnam conflict. "OK, I'm ready to do that," I said.

Bert had made some inquiries and an appointment for me the next day at the old central police headquarters on *Kungsholmen*. I was to bring my passport.

The interview was much longer and more detailed than I expected. A Swedish lieutenant, fluent in English, asked if he could tape the interview and I was OK with that. The lieutenant wanted to know how I had come to Sweden, why, and specifics of my background. I began with short and precise answers, but the lieutenant was thorough and probed every response. Soon, I began to relate in detail the history of my situation, from joining the Defense

Intelligence Agency (DIA) after university graduation to receiving a draft notice, joining the Washington, DC, Air National Guard, boot training, weapons training, and returning to work at the DIA. I described my growing opposition to the Vietnam conflict as a result of my work with Vietnamese tactical aerial photography and my analysis of the conflict's stupidity and questionable morality—how all of this had led me leave the DIA because I no longer wanted to be a participant in the war. Then, I described how I had been activated in January 1968, following the Pueblo Incident, posted to Myrtle Beach, South Carolina, and ordered to Vietnam. I described how, during my two-week furlough prior to posting, I had applied for a passport and booked a flight to Sweden.

After more than an hour, the interview was finally over. The Lieutenant asked me to wait and left the room. Ten minutes later he returned and said that my application had been approved and he put a stamp in my passport. "What does this say," I asked, pointing to the round stamp, inside of which the Lieutenant had written, "*diversearbetare.*"

"That is your work permit."

"OK, but what does this word mean?" I asked and pointed to *diversearbetare.*

"That means common laborer."

"What if I find a better job, can I do that?"

"Yes, but you will probably have to learn Swedish before that happens."

LETTERS

Wednesday, 24 July 1968

Dear Bruce,[4]

This is the first time I have sat down to write to anyone since returning from the hospital last Thursday. However, Mom didn't tell me until later . . . My immediate reaction was one of shock and fear. Shock at the realization of the

---

4   From Bruce's father, Bob Proctor in Norman, Oklahoma.

courage it took to make a decision with such life-long consequences and fear of the long arm of the CIA and FBI taking
possible defensive action against one in possession of classified information . . . Sgt. Bush called us from Myrtle Beach
on Friday reporting your non-appearance and apparently
trying to cover for you until the last minute. Rosemary's lawyer warned us against possible wire-tapping and not to give
out any information. It has meant a bit of worry and loss of
sleep here . . . However, since you now have a written postcard for anyone to see and since you say you are now legal, I
assume you no longer wish us to withhold any information.
Even though I felt shock and fear, I cannot say I was surprised. You have always been a person of ideals and strength
of conviction. I am glad you did not tell me, a naval reserve
captain, about it ahead of time. It would have made it doubly
difficult for me . . .

We are waiting for word from you on all the unanswered
questions. I guess you know what they are . . .

Love, Dad

Bruce, 2008-2009

I was cleared to receive top secret information through my job
with the DIA following university graduation. My father knew that
my absence would be seen as a possible compromise of classified
information, and I learned later that there was a furor over my leaving. Along with my father, I also felt fear. I dreamed that I was surrounded by FBI agents at night in an Iowa cornfield. I dreamt of
abduction from the streets of Stockholm by CIA agents. Paranoia
became a normal mode of perception, but, as the saying goes, "just
because you're afraid doesn't mean you don't have enemies."[5]

The DIA is the military intelligence coordinating agency for
the Joint Chiefs of Staff, the army, navy, air force, and marines. Sgt.
Bush was my immediate superior in the weapons shop at Myrtle

---

5   Bruce has probably paraphrased Joseph Heller's, "Just because you're para-
    noid doesn't mean they aren't after you." From *Catch-22*.

Beach Air Force Base where I had been stationed prior to my flight to Stockholm.

I grew up in a stable middle-class family in the 1950s and graduated from Bethesda-Chevy Chase High School, northwest of Washington, DC, in 1961. In the fall of 1961, my father, Bob, was sent to Bogotá, Colombia as part of the *Punto Quatro* foreign aid initiative, along with the rest of the family except for Dan, who was in the US Coast Guard Academy.

From Bogotá, I went to the University of North Carolina for the spring term of 1962 and then on to American University in the fall of that year, majoring in international relations and Latin American area studies.

Alan, 2014

Six months after Bruce left Bogotá for college, my sister went back to college and my parents and I moved to Panama City, Panama, where my father worked as an airport safety specialist for the US Government's Point Four (*Punto Quatro*) Plan that President Truman had instigated in 1950 to support science and technology in developing nations. Although we lived in Panama City, I went to high school in the Panama Canal Zone from 1962 to early 1964.

The Canal Zone, a 10-mile-wide thread of American colonialism in the center of the Isthmus of Panama, was administered by the US Government. This area had been under a lease agreement dating from 1904 when Teddy Roosevelt carried a big stick. In 1977, President Jimmy Carter signed a treaty with Panama that gave the Panamanians control of the canal starting in 2000.

For years there had been an understanding that the Americans in the Zone would fly both the US and Panamanian flags in public places. This arrangement disgruntled many Zonians—as the Canal Zone Americans were called. Riots broke out early in 1964 when students at my Canal Zone high school failed to fly the Panamanian flag alongside the star and stripes. Mark German, an army friend, who had Zonian license plates (and with whom both Bruce and Rosemary communicated by letter while in Sweden) was nearly killed when rioters surrounded his car. As he said, "I put it in reverse and got the hell out of there."

The US Government moved our family into the Tivoli Hotel when it was apparent it wasn't safe to return to our Panama City apartment. The hotel bordered the city and the Zone; its hotel balcony had been sandbagged. I dug bullets out of the exterior wall of our suite. We were soon shipped stateside.

Bruce, 2008–2009

While in university, when I realized that I tended toward the claustrophobic, I joined a cave crawling (spelunking) club and spent weekends in western Virginia breathing the moist, cool air of caves. Some were old mines, worked by slaves for nitrates to support the Confederate cause. I got over my claustrophobia when the club was exploring a sewer cave. Sewer caves are holes in the ground into which rainwater flows, with no known outlets. After a bit, I was deep into this sewer, flat on my back, head down, clawing my way along a downward-sloping tube in the rock. It was too tight to crawl, and I had to crab my way along and keep going; there was no way to back up, feet first uphill. Besides, there was someone else in front of me and someone else behind me. It took all my self-control to still the rising panic. All of us had been assured by the expedition leader that there was a way out of this tube at the other end; and, sure enough, there was. I thought I owed my life to the accuracy of this fact, but also thought it was foolish to take a bunch of amateurs down a potentially blind lead to a sewer's grave. I quit cave-crawling after this trip. Fear is sometimes justified.

Toward the end of university, I studied Tae Kwon Do. Prior to this, I had nightmares of being attacked at night by a gang while with a date. I was overwhelmed and beaten; she was raped. I was a green belt before the nightmares went away and I quit training. I had learned to control fear of physical attack, look upon aggression with dispassion, act reflexively, not fear the possibility of death or injury, and control aggression with necessary and only sufficient force. Overkill was to be avoided. A black belt member of the *dojang* from the Metropolitan Police was reprimanded by his employer for the use of unnecessary force in subduing a drunk. The black belt then had to stand before the *dojang* and apologize for wrongful behavior.

As I approached graduation in June of 1965, I was encouraged by one professor to go on to graduate school with scholarships at Cornell in Latin American studies. Instead, I wanted to see the "real world" and get a job.

Alan, 2014

Watching the news on TV in late 1963, I witnessed Thích Quảng Đức's body burning in a Vietnamese street. He was protesting the repressive policies the Catholic Diem wielded over the South Vietnamese government at the time. Buddhist monks and nuns nationwide wanted to fly the banned traditional Buddhist flag. Duc's death—his saffron robe and blackened, supplicant arms crumbling within the flames of his own immolation—had haunted my high school dreams for weeks. In late 1965, during my senior year in high school, a Quaker named Norman Morrison set himself on fire below Secretary of Defense Robert McNamara's office to protest the Vietnam War. Morrison had died off-camera, but surely no less horribly than the monk.

Bruce, 2008-2009

So, in the spring of 1965 I was recruited by the DIA to become a military intelligence analyst. That spring, a long-time roommate, Peter H, told me the DIA was looking for me, recruiters were on campus and wanted to talk with me. I had not noticed their announcements on bulletin boards. So, I went off to meet them. The interview was a bit strange: he asked me what I had studied but seemed to know the answers I gave. He offered me a job. "Doing what?" I asked.

"You know," he said. Although I did not know, the offer was very attractive, starting as a GS-11, I would be promoted to GS-12 after a year and could get a full-time master's degree in intelligence research and analysis from American University, at that pay grade, with full salary, tuition, and books covered. Following that, a promotion to GS-13 and . . .

But that did not stop the Selective Service Administration in their pursuit to draft me; they sent me a letter and I went, took the psychological and aptitude tests, bent over for the physical, wished I'd put blood in my urine and lied to the psychiatrist that I could think of no reason why I might not be fit for duty in the US Army.

I should have told the shrink that the thought of killing others offended me but, under certain circumstance, sure, if they are not subdued by sufficient force, they intend to kill you and have the means and opportunity, one must defend oneself—a fine point, under the circumstances.

The DIA sent me to the Military Intelligence School, newly established, the first class. But the draft was getting close and I looked for other options. Father Bob got me a physical and subsequent reporting time to go to Pensacola, Florida, for navy flight training, not as a pilot, but as an "air observer," the guy sitting in the back seat of the F-4 Phantom fighter who worked the radar, navigation, and armament circuits for the pilot. I remember thinking that I really did not want to napalm peasants and gave this opportunity a pass. I opted instead for the Washington, DC, Air National Guard as an enlisted person. They were gearing up and taking new recruits for their F-100 Super Saber squadron. The deal was five years of service of one weekend a month, technical training, and two weeks' active duty once a summer following boot camp.

So, I took my motorcycle southeast out into the country to Andrews Air Force Base on a sunny fall day and was directed at the gate to the National Guard administrative offices. They were interested and recruiting, so I did some applications, was later notified and went out again to be sworn in by a captain, fingers crossed behind my back, and given a reporting date. The captain didn't seem to know the enlistment drill and the clerks also appeared new to the procedures. Little did I know then that they were preparing orders for battle-readiness status.

Basically, I put in time, waiting for my date with boot camp near San Antonio, Texas. We were issued uniforms, given a haircut, and marched up and down the parking lot of the administration building. I qualified on the M-1 and we were given an extensive battery of intelligence tests—I scored in the 90th percentiles on all of them.

"So, what do you want to do?" asked the sergeant, leafing through the test results.

"I want to be a cook," I answered, repeating the answer I had rehearsed with Ken P, my buddy from the DIA who had also enlisted in the DC Air National Guard. This was the trade that we had discovered had the shortest technical training time and was also in low demand in Vietnam.

"You can do better than that," said the sergeant.

"No, I want to be a cook," I said.

"Just let me review with you some other alternatives that are open to you, just listen." I nodded. I didn't want to get into an argument.

"There's training in avionics, the electronics of the aircraft, the radar, instruments, and navigational aids."

"Where is that . . . how long is the training?" I asked.

"It's in Biloxi, Mississippi—it lasts eight months."

I thought of swamps, mosquitoes, heat, and humidity. "No, I don't think so."

"Then there are armaments—you learn to load bombs, rockets and missiles; you troubleshoot and maintain armament circuits."

"Where and how long?"

"Denver, Colorado, for three months."

I paused. Denver was where an old girlfriend lived—she was interested in me and I was interested in her. "Tell me more about armaments."

Technical school would start immediately after boot camp in San Antonio. From there I'd fly to Denver and be back in Washington, DC, in May 1966.

When I later saw Ken and told him what I'd done, he couldn't believe it. "What were you thinking?" he asked. I told him about the girlfriend in Denver. "Well, I'm going to be a cook," he said.

So, I went to boot camp for Christmas and in January on to Denver for tactical weapons training. In the meantime, the girlfriend there had become engaged. She invited me to dinner with her fiancé and I never saw her again. So much for matters of the heart.

I returned to Washington, DC, from Denver in the summer of 1966, went back to my job at the DIA, and was glad I would not be drafted. I was then rotated between short-term jobs in various units

for exposure to a variety of intelligence activities, including management of covert human intelligence (spies behind the iron curtain).
The director gave me a tour of the large, cube-shaped building south
of the Pentagon.

"You do not want to work here," he said. "The pressure from
senior levels to get information is unreasonable. Yes, it can be done,
but often at very high risk to our operatives. Sometimes the requests
are trivial, but the risks of compromise are great for what they want,
up the line." He looked upward and rolled his eyes in supplication to
some unreasonable god. "If they would just leave us alone to develop
the networks, we could provide invaluable information . . . but it
takes time . . . and patience. In the meantime, our people are caught
and die."

DEPARTMENT OF DEFENSE
DEFENSE INTELLIGENCE AGENCY
WASHINGTON. D. C. 20301

SECRET   FOR OFFICIAL USE ONLY

EXCLUDED FROM AUTOMATIC REGRADING

DOD DIR 5200-10 DOES NOT APPLY

NO FOREIGN DISSEM

Page ___/___ of ___/___ pages

Copy ___/___ of ___/___ copies

N/A   WHEN

STAMPED FROM CLASSIFIED

MATERIAL

25 Nov 66

Lt. (JG) Daniel Huntington and Mrs. Judith Proctor
164 Wentworth, Apt. 9
Charleston, S.C.

Dear Mr. Proctor:

It has come to the attention of this department that you and
your wife are conspiring to achieve happiness outside the
encompassing bounds of the Department of Defense. You are
being put on notice that this is an impossibility.

We once had a case where one of our own decided that "the whole
world was but a stage, and we the actors upon it," to paraphrase
a well-known subversive. As we all know, Mr. Proctor, the truth
of the matter is that the whole stage is a world, and nobody else
is important. As you know the only REAL stage is the Department.
Therefore, it would behoove you to reconsider your decision,
and to stick by those who really know what your soul is all about.
I do not need to remind you of the power we can bring to bear
to assist you in seeing the justice and righteousness of this
course of action. We have submitted your name for a purple heart.
Final action only awaits word that you have signed reenlistment
papers.

Do not forget us, Mr. Proctor; we will never forget you.

SINCERELY,

Horation O. Hornblower

P.S. Please excuse my poor typing, but letters of this personal
a nature, I usually type myself.

FOR OFFICIAL USE ONLY   SECRET   NO FOREIGN DISSEM

Written on official Department of Defense stationery to his brother Dan (A U.S.
Naval Lieutenant), Bruce's letter ridicules the DOD.

Alan, 2014

In the fall of 1966, I had a college deferment as an incoming freshman. Nonetheless, a week before I started school, I was ordered by the Norman, Oklahoma, draft board to catch a bus into Oklahoma City for a pre-induction army physical. When I boarded the bus, a man wearing khaki pants ordered me to "take charge" of the other passengers during the drive. Perhaps I was chosen because he knew I had a college deferment. At any rate, once I had murmured my consent—without any knowledge of what was expected of me—the man got off the bus and signaled the driver to leave.

Most of the travelers were my age: recent high school graduates. No one talked; we peered out of the bus window at the redundant landscape. I bounced on the badly padded seat and thought of the conversation I should, but wouldn't have with my bus-mates:

"Hello future murderers and cannon fodder! I'm Alan Proctor, with a college deferment. The gentleman with the monotone voice and stick up his ass told me your butts belong to me for the next twenty miles. What's say we all stand up, join hands, and sing the chorus of the 'I feel Like I'm Going to Die' rag by Country Joe and the Fish? You all know it!"

But perhaps they didn't know it. What they knew was that for many of them, Vietnam would be in their near future. And me? In two months, I'd be an incoming freshman at a Quaker college in Indiana majoring in English.

Bruce, 2008-2009

At the DIA, in the analysis section for Central America and the Caribbean, I was schooled to see that the communist threat was everywhere, egged on by that scoundrel, Castro. While there, I briefed the under secretary of state on the communist menace in Nicaragua. I didn't believe there was much of a threat. Top secret reports from the CIA, which had infiltrated the party up to the executive level, suggested that they were up to no good, but they had only 123 members and the CIA source mostly reported on who was sleeping with whom. Their capabilities to mount any rebellion against President Somoza seemed remote.

But, the line was the threat—how else to justify the sizeable US military mission in Managua and the sale of US weapons to him—not to mention the United Fruit Company and other multinationals active in their economy? True, Somoza was a tricky character—a report from the US ambassador on a meeting with him regarding concerns in the United States with his electoral processes yielded this response: "But, we don't do anything differently than they do in the delta parishes of Louisiana." He was interested, however, in the findings of a US armaments survey group: in the cellar of the presidential palace, old munitions were discovered whose explosion could be triggered by a slight jolt, the TNT having crystallized from age. They also found improper storage techniques and hoarding of dangerous igniters in the proximity of explosives.

"Of course," said President Somoza, "if you want to help me clean up and resupply, I would be most interested."

I began to prepare an exit route. If I requested specialized training, I could get it if I had decided on a career path. I had liked Denver and wanted to return. They had an aerial photographic interpretation course there that lasted five months and I would stay in the Bachelor Officer Quarters and get a *per diem* on top of my wage—making it possible to quit with some cash in my pocket.

Following the five months of training back at the same air force base near Denver where I had studied weapons, I joined a special aerial photographic interpretation unit in Washington, DC. The cans of film taken by the reconnaissance version of the F-4 Phantom would be flown PDQ to Washington from the flight decks of the carriers cruising in the Gulf of Tonkin. I would scroll through the film with a map at hand showing the approximate flight path of the jet and the designated bomb targets with their numbers noted. My job was to detect any changes in damage to these targets on a form. With my 10-power glass, looking at the images on the positive print of the negatives, I noticed a cluster of bomb craters, almost hidden under the trees of a small village. Checking my map, I found that this village was not a designated bomb target.

The next morning over coffee I read *The Washington Post* story "President Johnson Repeats Claim that US Is Bombing Only Military Targets."

Hmmm . . . I thought, *well, if the damage doesn't get reported, then it must not exist.*

Back at work, I viewed and analyzed photography shot over Cambodia and Laos. The mere existence of these special analysis units was classified. The administration claimed it was not bombing either country.

For me, this presented a moral quandary. Since I was cleared for top secret information, to tell anyone what I thought I knew to be true would be a federal offense under the secrets act, punishable by potentially lengthy prison time. By the summer of 1967, I was tired of the lies, tired of being a part of the killing machine, and I quit the DIA.

That fall, I enrolled in graduate school at the University of Maryland in American studies and got a part-time job teaching high school civics and US history. In December, I married Rosemary Wolf, a fellow graduate from American University in international relations.

The year of 1968 did not start well. In January, my [Air National Guard] unit was activated on the pretext of an increased threat from North Korea following the "Pueblo Incident" (when a North Korean gunboat boarded and captured a US "fishing trawler" that had been rehabilitated into a covert signals intelligence-gathering ship). In truth, the United States was experiencing manpower shortages in Vietnam and the F-100s of my reserve unit would come in handy for bombing and strafing.

By the summer of 1968, both Martin Luther King Jr. and Bobby Kennedy would be dead. The men most needed in the squadron (not including cooks) were transferred to the air force base near Myrtle Beach, South Carolina; Rosemary joined me there. By late June, the unit was ready, and many received orders to go to Vietnam, including me, most of the other armament mechanics, and other trades in short supply—along with the planes and the pilots. Before leaving, all of those with orders to 'Nam had to qualify on the new M-16 assault rifle, much praised by gunnery sergeants. So, in the company of my buddies from armament, along with tires, hydraulics, engine, and aero-systems electronics guys, we all took a bus to the rifle range.

Some of the guys from rural Maryland who were hunters had heard of the M-16. One of them expounded, "The M-16 is wicked, man, lightweight, little recoil, can be fully automatic. The bullet is small but it has a magnum load, so it has a high velocity. If it hits an arm, it will shatter it, spraying shrapnel that kills. It has excellent accuracy down range."

"Sounds like a dum-dum bullet," I said. "That's outlawed under the Geneva Convention."

"Same effect, but not the same," he said.

"How so?"

"Dum-dums are soft-headed or cross-hatched to explode on contact, but the M-16 has a steel metal jacket. It's the velocity that makes it behave like a dum-dum, but it's legal."

So, we were lined up behind the firing positions, a tunnel effect down range into the side of a hill, the firing positions canopied against the setting sun to the left. The gunnery sergeant had two assistants who stood to the side, arms folded.

"You are here today" said the gunny, "to qualify on the M-16 assault rifle. This is it," he said, twirling to a present arms. "You will learn to use this weapon to kill your enemies, the Viet Cong—" He mumbled something about whoever else may come into your line of fire before continuing. "Take this rifle and hold it in front of you." The assistants passed out the weapons. "You will look at the safety and ensure that it is on—you will note that the breach is open. When you insert a clip into the bottom hole, like this," he snapped one into place, "and release the squeezes for the breach, it will chamber your first round."

Squeezes? I thought. Several others chuckled.

"Yes, assholes," said the gunny, "you will die if you don't do it right. The two clips protruding back . . . squeeze them together like this." As he did so, he sent the slide forward with a click that sounded dangerous. "We are going to fire this weapon from three positions: prone, sitting, and standing. Now take your weapons to the firing line."

We all lay down (with the assistants kicking some legs into the proper position). "Prone position," said the gunny. "Don't look at me, asshole, face the fucking target. Down there is the enemy," pointing toward the base of the hill. "You have a box of ammunition on your right-hand side. There are three clips of ten cartridges. You will fire one clip in each of the three positions. You will be scored on hits

inside the bull's-eye on your target. You must hit the target to qualify. If you don't, you will come back tomorrow, and I do not want to
see any of you ever again—but, if I do—you'll be sorry." He paused.
"Now load and lock—line up the sights—release the safety—fire
when ready—empty your clip."

The "phew" of high-velocity bullets began to sound around me.
I peered through the sights at the concentric black and white circles
on the chest of the human straw target. It took concentration to
settle the sights on the target. *What the fuck*, I thought, pulling the
trigger. I did not see where the round went and emptied my clip into
the paper enemy. I noticed the recoil was not as bad as the M-1, just a
friendly slap to the right shoulder with each round, like a big brother
punching and saying, "Hey, how are you doing?"

As we settled into the sitting position, the gunny said, "If the
Cong storm the base and the marines can't stop them, you will use
this weapon to kill as many of them as possible, before they kill you.
They may come at you through the mess hall, around the corner of a
hanger, across the runways and aprons, right into your lap . . . do you
want to die? Hit that target in the center and blow them away." I was
finding the litany of kill or be killed a bit repetitive.

"Now—in the standing position—keep aiming down range, asshole—squeeze it off after you hold your breath and between heart-
beats. This is the test—kill those gooks."

I squeezed off seven rounds and then hesitated. I turned my neck
around to the right, pretending to loosen the stress, spotting the
three sergeants patrolling behind the firing line, unarmed. I looked
forward again and began to take aim.

I had a strange sensation of being out of my body, looking down
on myself from just under the canopy that shaded the firing line
from the late-afternoon sun. I could see myself turning, firing my last
three rounds into the gunny and assistants. From there I could not
see an escape route that ended without my death.

Others along the line had finished firing. The gunny was by my
side. "Finish firing," he yelled into my left ear. I finished and qualified, went home to Rosemary, and told her the story.

That night, I had a dream. Again, I could see myself from above,
in my bed in Myrtle Beach, and an apparition of light approached
above me, coming forward, taking on form, resolving into a sparkling

angel, in white gown with shimmering sequins, a crown of lights, and holding a wand—glittering like a sparkler—like the Witch of the East in *The Wizard of OZ*. She seemed to be saying, "Everything will be fine . . . you do not want to go there."

The next morning, I remembered this dream, told Rosemary about it and she said, "We could go to Sweden." But first I had two weeks' leave, standard practice before an overseas posting. We returned to DC and I applied for a passport and bought a plane ticket to Stockholm from New York. Then, Rosemary and I visited my parents in Norman, Oklahoma. I was not aware that Canada provided refuge, but I knew Sweden did after press reports of the "Intrepid Four" and others who had been granted humanitarian asylum.

Alan, 2014

During 1967 in the spring of my freshman year, Timothy Zimmer, an upperclassman refused—in the middle of his studies— to continue his college deferment for reasons of conscience and left school. As an eligible young male, he was ordered to report for duty in the army under Paragraph 462 of Title 50, Appendix, of the US Selective Service Code. He refused and was sentenced to three years in prison. In his statement to the court he said: ". . . The state may prohibit violence and murder, but it *may not compel the individual to become violent, to murder* (emphasis mine)." He served just under two years and came back to Earlham as the spring 1969 semester began. He was as an oddity to some, something of a celebrity to others. I once asked him how prison changed him, and he said, "I don't like closed doors." His book, *Letters of a C.O. from Prison* (The Judson Press, 1969), is heart-wrenching.

In the summer of 1968, when Bruce went AWOL, I was working in New Orleans as the doorman for the Bourbon Orleans Hotel. It was the summer between my sophomore and junior year at Earlham. New Orleans was as hot as I remembered Panama, but unlike Panama, all the buildings were air conditioned. The heat slapped me every time I went outside.

I knew Bruce had worked for the government at the Defense Intelligence Agency and had joined the Air National Guard which, at that time, was not slated for overseas service. He lived in different and rarefied air. As his little brother, my life revolved around staying in college to avoid being drafted and—if I were lucky—getting laid. It wasn't until the draft lottery began that fall that the war took on a new and ominous reality for me. I had a college deferment for the time being, but what would happen when I graduated? A soccer player at school told me he'd enlist. He said he wanted to protect America. What, I wondered, did fighting in Vietnam have to do with protecting America?

A senior from Antioch College told me about the American Civil Liberties Union. ACLU attorney William Kunstler advised draft-eligible men to go to Canada or Sweden. The senior told me, "Swedish babes are hot," before recounting an evening of unbridled sex with Inga.

I acquired a copy of the *Draft Resister's Guide to Settlement in Canada*, a thin chapbook printed on bad paper. It seemed humorously clandestine: ". . . when you arrive in Montreal, ask for Mr. Earhart at the Unitarian Church on Boul De Maisonneuve. Make sure you are alone with him before beginning any conversation about your situation . . ." I read Norman Mailer's *Armies of the Night* which chronicled the story of Don Batey who took refuge from the draft in a Methodist church: "I am a young human being struggling to cope with a bewildering world . . ." My Earlham classmate Timothy Zimmer, who spent nearly two years in jail for refusing induction, must have known how he felt; Mr. Batey was sentenced to four years for draft evasion.

After the Viet Cong's Tet Offensive in January of 1968, I had briefly considered changing my major from English to political science. How could anybody (except the idiots at the highest levels of government) think America would win this war? The press had quoted the marine commandant, a General David Shoup, who called the administration's rationale for fighting "poppycock." Shoup had probably said, "Bullshit." The Vietnam War, as the general put it, was a civil conflict between the Vietnamese nationals and the corrupt crooks in Saigon. Unfortunately, the United States was backing the criminals in Saigon. Poly-sci was a mind-blower.

Lyndon Johnson told the nation he "would not seek, nor accept another term" as president. I had grimly concluded that the pronouncement vindicated the anti-war movement.

The political vacuum quickly filled. The ill-fated Robert Kennedy became a candidate. The poet-politician, Eugene McCarthy, for whom I campaigned, joined the race. On the Republican side, the segregationist George Wallace chose retired Air Force General Curtis LeMay as his running mate. LeMay's military strategy was unequivocal: ". . . Bomb 'em back to the Stone Age, use nuclear weapons if necessary." Good thing the Wallace–LeMay ticket lost.

In 1968, Martin Luther King Jr. and Robert Kennedy were assassinated in April and June, respectively. For days, the college was stunned. In May, the Berrigan brothers, both poets and Catholic priests, broke into the Catonsville, Maryland, draft office. They napalmed 600 draft files. "I went to Catonsville," Daniel Berrigan said, "to burn some papers because the burning of children is inhuman and unbearable." Kunstler defended them. They were sentenced to three-and-a half years.

The late poet Bill Knott visited our campus for a poetry reading. At the time, he wrote under the pen name of Saint Geraud. I tacked the two concluding lines from a poem in his book *The Naomi Poems: Corpse and Beans* to the foot of my bed. The lines are from "Nuremburg, USA."

> . . . If bombing children is preserving peace, then
> my fucking you is a war-crime.

Chapter Two
Our Roots Are in the Sky

LETTERS

July 24, 1968
(Posted in Washington, DC, from Rosemary Proctor)

Dear Mom and Dad Proctor,

Received your envelope with letter, etc. Your letter made me very, very happy. It makes this thing so much easier for Bruce and me, when we know that you understand so well...

Bruce will be so glad to hear from Peter H. (first letter since Dec.). I read it—Peter is happy in Japan, studying language, history, and Zen. In the letter, he said that he and a friend went to stay at a monastery and were the third and fourth Westerners, respectively, to receive permission to stay there in its 700-year history—an honor not even accorded to Allen Watts, apparently. Peter is also planning a trip to India, to begin I'm not sure when, and after some time there will begin to hitch westward. All of this very vague with no certain timetable.

I just finished talking with Bruce. He is fine, cheerful. Called because he had received a letter I wrote last Saturday when I was quite upset and afraid. He also wanted to consult about apartments; apparently, he had been offered several and it is a choice between one in town for $120 (which is a bit much for Sweden), or one of several out of town for less (but we would also have transportation costs that way, train or subway or both, and that's an added expense). I could only tell him to use his own judgment. The one in town is furnished, at least. It was so good to talk with him, as you can imagine, after I got over my first panic that something was wrong. The connection was fantastic. We only spoke for a few minutes, and that about business.

He said two letters were in the mail, containing all the business details, so I will forward them, or write to you when I receive them.

Love, Rosemary

July 27, 1968

My Darling Bruce,[6]

After you said "goodbye" to me and we watched the plane, almost out of sight, I had the feeling that it was not true—that you could not be going to Vietnam. Your attitude at home was not one of belligerence—as it should have been. And quiet acceptance has never been your way.

When I got your letter through Rosemary, Bob was in the hospital, and I decided for several reasons not to tell him about it until he had had a few good nights of rest, which he needed. He was at home on Friday the 19th when Sgt. Bush called to say you had not come in for processing, and he asked me when you arrived here and when you left—and how. I told him, as far as I knew, you were on your way back to Myrtle Beach. He called back to tell me not to worry—you had not turned in your key for the apartment and that the military police had been to the apartment. We have had no further communication from the military. Of course, Bob had to know then, and we both wrote Rosemary and talked to her on the phone about Sgt. Bush's call. He was probably trying to cover for you until the last minute, according to

---

6   Posted in Norman, Oklahoma, from Bruce's mother, Ella Mae Proctor.

Bob, so I called Rosemary the next morning [and told her] not to worry too much about it, and we all decided that we would not talk about it or give any information to anyone. We still have told no one and will not until Rosemary is safely with you. I did write Carol[7], because you did not mention telling her, but I only wrote yesterday, and she does not yet know exactly where you are by address. I think Rosemary told Dan and Alan to keep quiet about it. Bob got a letter from Dan written on a huge "get-well" card to say what we all felt—that "Bruce knows where his values are and has the courage to act on them. There are not many of his kind."

As for me, my emotions are so mixed—but the greatest one is relief. You may remember that months ago I wrote you not to go to Vietnam under any conditions. That was right after I had a very real and terrible dream which I lived with for days before I told Bob. I think when Bob remembered that night of weeping, he was also greatly relieved, and that it made it easier for both of us to know that the alternative which you chose meant life for you. I could not tell you about it when you were here—all I could say was that if I were a young man, I would not go—and perhaps you were glad to hear this.[8]

Naturally, these last weeks have been filled with anxiety—that you were really safe; that you would not be accepted for asylum (we heard on the TV that some American boys were not accepted there); that we would not have to evade the questions; that Rosemary could safely join you, etc. But I have been at comparative peace since your card came saying you were legal. I try not to let myself think of the long years of separation or the adjustment you must make there with the knowledge that you cannot return. I am so proud of you! Not to make compromises with your true beliefs, even at a great sacrifice, is a rare kind of courage. I know it was not

---

7   Bruce's sister

8   Ella Mae had other uncanny premonitions: the correct location in a dream of an uncle undergoing an emergency appendectomy, and a last-minute warning to her husband Bob not to board a train which, as it turned out, derailed and killed several passengers.

fear of death, but fear of not being able to live while taking part in killing. There are thousands of young men who have been forced to seek an alternative to taking part in this immoral and unjust war, and my greatest sadness is for the loss of them to this county where they are needed to help correct the great wrongs here. I only pray that someday there may be a legal way for all of them to return.

You are very lucky to have friends there and to have a place to go to immediately. Rosemary sent us a couple of articles from *The New York Times*, one about deserters there. It said 55 to 60 Americans have received permanent residence permits and asylum on humanitarian grounds in Sweden and that perhaps 50 are active in the American Deserters Committee. I assume you will not become associated with the committee which that paper said had recently lost the sympathy of one of their earlier [Swedish] supporters, Bertil Svanstrom. You are probably wise just to fade into Swedish life.

We talked to Rosemary last night, and she says she is leaving this Tuesday night and will be there Wednesday morning—perhaps even before this letter arrives. By now perhaps you have found an apartment. We are anxious to know details. Do you have to get a work permit? Are you studying the language yet? What type of job will be available for you there? And for Rosemary?

Bob is writing about money matters, etc. And Rosemary has all the mail which has been forwarded here. I assume by now that the US has been told that you are in asylum there—the TV said the other day that the 83rd American has just been granted asylum, and we wondered if that was you. Two others were denied. Perhaps we will hear nothing further from the military. I hope so. The authorities there would certainly have told them by now.

Dan is busy as usual, and Carol has moved into her new home . . . We hear little from Alan, but assume he is still a doorman at a hotel on Bourbon Street. Bob is getting along fine [after surgery] but needs to relax and rest for a month.

I live a daily prayer for you and for Rosemary. I love you for being exactly what you are.

Mom

Bruce, 2008-2009

The early morning sun was streaming in the window as the phone rang. Groggy, I focused on the bedside clock—4:00 a.m. Who would be calling at this hour? Tentatively, I picked up the phone—"Hello?"

Bert exclaimed, "Rise and shine, the day is wasting, let's go sailing."

"It's four o'clock," I moaned, though I could see that it was a beautiful day.

"So? Swedes like to play when the sun shines. I could pick you up in half an hour."

"OK," I said.

Bert kept his boat at a small marina east of Stockholm on the road to Saltsjobaden. By 5:00 a.m. we were on the road with very little traffic once out in the countryside. With my boating experience from East Hampton, I was ready to play the deckhand. I cast off the lines and assisted with the sails. Bert set a course east out of the main channel, before a following wind. Around noon, Bert pulled into the lee of a small island, a tongue of water among cliffs where the wind could not penetrate, glassy calm, and I threw out the anchor on the command of the skipper. Bert pulled a small stove out of the cabin and on deck started two eggs boiling. When they were finished, Bert cooled them by dipping the pot over the side in the clear, calm water.

I looked around when Bert said, "Damn" (*javla*, in Swedish). The two eggs, still in the pot, clearly seen at perhaps 20 feet, under the keel, lay on the bottom beneath the boat. "We have to get them," said Bert.

I tested the water. "Chilly," I said. The boat went slowly through a pendulum motion, swinging on the anchor rope back and forth across the pot with its two white orbs, gazing at us gazing at them, over the side. Ever the Viking, Bert stripped down, dived in, and retrieved the pot, eggs intact. The lunch of potatoes cooked in dill, smoked herring, eggs, flatbread, and butter (*smör*) tasted wonderful under the brilliant sun, amongst the clear water, with granite cliffs and pine trees around, the flat smell of abundant water, a hint of heather upon the wind.

I did not think much about Sgt. Bush back in Myrtle Beach, South Carolina, and his problems locating me. He was the one who recommended reading *Catch-22*, which I did while still at Andrews Air Force Base outside DC. I never finished it, but Sgt. Bush told me that the "hero" in the end deserts to Sweden. By this time, as well, I knew that an old high school friend, Parker S., had gone to Sweden after being activated in early 1968. He was with a navy reserve squadron of fighter jets located in the hangar next to ours at Andrews.

LETTERS

1 August 1968
Stockholm

Norman Man Gets Asylum

STOCKHOLM (UPI)—A 25-year-old Norman, Okla. resident, Bruce Stevens Proctor, was among 10 U. S. deserters granted asylum in Sweden, the Aliens Commission revealed Friday. (Aug. 2)

Mrs. Robert H. Proctor, his mother, would only say, "I'm sorry, we do not want to give out any information at this time. The public will have to get along on the brief announcement that has been made. We want to keep this as private as possible."

A total of 92 U. S. servicemen have now been granted asylum in Sweden.

Aug. 3 '68
Oklahoma Journal

Dear Mom & Dad,

Just a short note to tell you that Rosemary arrived safely with all your mail to her. I think it would be very ill-advised to tell the authorities or anyone who might tell the authorities of my whereabouts, a postcard notwithstanding. When I said I was legal, it meant only that I'm legally registered with the police. The Aliens Commission has yet to pass favorably on my application for asylum. I don't expect to hear from them until the end of August. In the interim, I don't see the sense in offering the United States the opportunity to exert

Newspaper clipping from the August 3, 1968, *Oklahoma Journal* announcing Bruce's asylum in Sweden.

diplomatic pressure. This they cannot do without verification of my being here; and if they're in the dark, so much the better. In other words, I am still legally in limbo. There have been examples of a refusal of application. I don't know the circumstances, but don't want to take any chances. I have not contacted or talked to any groups, reporters, strangers, etc., about my position for these reasons.

I am already beginning to suspect that I have been living an alien existence in the USA for 25 years, and that all along I was born to be a Swede. I'm certainly proud to be here and find being a European much more comfortable. One doesn't have to apologize for one's opinions. Diversity and toleration are recognized facts of life. Anyway, I'm happy and have no regrets.

Bruce

Alan, 2014

In 1975, this poem was accepted for publication by *New Letters*, the literary journal which David Ray (who wrote the preface to this book) edited.

Lure

I remove the hook gently as if your mouth
were caught in a lie.
You must have wondered
what rare cloud
bellied out into your world,
the smooth dinghy bottom deceiving.
I cut you open for bait,
work along the stripes in your side
for meat that clings to the hook.
The waters flesh light and dark, a cold morning.
My next-door neighbor died in the war,
my brother deserted.
I fish like a crazed sea dog

until the sun disappears,
clouds slice their wrists.
Forgive us, fish, for luring you here.
How can we explain the pride
our lives require?

LETTERS

1 August 1968
Stockholm

Dear Alan,

Little did I suspect that someday . . . The karma was a long one, and a hard one. If I know you, you'll be smart enough to avoid it.

This is a truly beautiful country: bare rock outcroppings attest to the recently departed glaciers. The whole country from the northern coniferous forests to the glacial lake region responds to the long, warm summer days. The clean air is filled with the smell of wild flowers, the sky is deep blue, punctuated by light cumulus clouds. The Swedes are on vacation and everybody gets a month off, so Stockholm is filled with tourists while the natives retire to summer homes by clean glacial lakes or on the fjord-notched coast. Many go camping or tour Europe. It's a country of sun worshipers since the winter days are so short. All the park benches face south. Have you seen Swedish modern furniture? Many things have the same elegance and taste which comes from a tradition of workmanship and maximum use of native materials. The sailboats, houses, subway stations, street signs, furniture, and even the landscape denote a reflective, harmonious consciousness of the whole. There is no need for escape into some other meaningful reality; it surrounds you . . .[9]

. . . I am enrolled in Swedish courses four days a week and have been seeing the sights, been sailing, walking, looking,

---

9   In the coming months, nearly every proclamation of Swedish perfection began to wear thin as Bruce's utopian exile became a dystopian reality.

reading, writing, and thinking. It is a better place for me and I have no regrets; my bitterness has dissipated through the clear atmosphere and my opinions, which I always considered rational, are here a reality; for the Swedes made a choice in favor of the rational many years ago. Health insurance and hospitalization are free; cities are planned, there are no slums; there is no socially or politically manifest fear or hate; foreign policy is neutral. The police are civil servants. Domestic politics is so sane that it bores most Swedes. Perhaps I am lucky that I did not grow up here, for what the Swede finds boring, I find fascinating; what causes them to drink (there is a drinking problem), I see only as the internalization of asocial behavior. Perhaps the Swedes know this also. The consciousness of Ingmar Bergman is a national consciousness, one that I don't share (although I did several years ago). I find that the country offers all that you can expect three-dimensional reality to offer. The other dimensions are personal and transcendent, not social or political. This realization may lead me into a radical shift in endeavor here in Sweden. I have little interest in the academic realities, because here they are also social and political realities (what a contrast with the US). In short, I feel that as a nation, Sweden has gone just about as far as western rationalism and humanism can take any country. Having arrived, the Swedes are left without purpose. I overstate the case, but only because it contrasts so remarkably with the United States. Yes, I am beginning to grow outward just sitting here drinking coffee, writing to you, and wondering how you are in New Orleans, that center of Negro self-expression under the heel.

Write soon, love, Bruce

August 12, 1968
Stockholm

Dear Mom and Dad,[10]

Today we received official notice of our asylum, also work permits. Everything is fine. They have instituted a new regulation that provides asylum for three months, and then we apply again and go for a year. There is nothing to worry about.

We met another deserter on Saturday morning. He had been in contact with other deserters and attended the group meetings . . . there have been quite a few problems. Most of the Americans are on welfare and not making any attempt to learn Swedish or get jobs. In addition, many have been politically active in an embarrassing way. Several went to the International Youth Conference in Sofia—they cannot return to Sweden. There are apparently about 100 deserters in France—they cannot get work permits. Also, about 100 are AWOL in Belgium and awaiting a chance to come here. We hear—it is hard to know how true—that many go AWOL in Vietnam and hide out in the jungle waiting for a chance to make connections and get to Japan. Several have recently arrived, but this is terribly dangerous and costs a lot . . .

Love, Rosemary

---

10   From Rosemary to Bob and Ella Mae Proctor.

16 August 1968
Stockholm

Dear Dad and Mom,

I suppose the news has reached the shop[11] and been greeted by not too much surprise. My nickname was Ho Chi Minh. They renew the work and residence permits in December for three months, then six months, then a year, etc. The policy is flexible and varies with the individual case, but nobody has been known to be deported except on grounds of previous criminality, that is, if they came to Sweden to escape prosecution for a crime. The language lessons are coming along fine; the government pays our rent, travel, and other minor expenses while I'm looking for work. A friend offered to get me work in a factory, but I would have to quit taking Swedish, so I declined. My class is from 1500–2100 hours, so I can only work in the morning. The prospects are good for jobs teaching businessmen. Swedish is not difficult. The structure is closer to English than any other foreign language. The pronunciation and spelling are bitchy, but that just takes time. You don't want to learn Swedish; it's useless unless you live here, and everybody speaks English anyway; that's one thing that makes it hard to learn the language—all the Swedes want to practice their English with you.

Love, Bruce

---

11 The weapons shop at the air force base in Myrtle Beach, SC, where Bruce was a crew chief.

Bruce, 2008–2009

Bert made some inquiries about foreign workers' language training and I signed up in the fall of 1968. I was surprised to find that while in full-time training I would receive a modest living allowance, funds to buy a monthly pass on the subway and buses, free tuition, and books.

The Swedes were definitely being progressive in this area as early as 1968 when it was a relatively new program. I was also surprised to see the investment made in computers, a dedicated teacher for six hours per day, and the small class size. I attended a renovated facility near Slussen in Soder for six weeks. Classmates included both sexes from Greece, Turkey, Spain, and even Italy. I applied myself, but the language did not come easily. I often confused Swedish with Spanish, the other foreign language that I had struggled to learn in high school and university.

I lusted after the instructor, a very together young woman, blonde, in charge of this class. She had such a perfect accent, timing, and intonation—simple sayings came alive to her cadence of certitude—do like I do and say like I say—that was the message—a double reinforcement, if there ever was one.

Bruce (right) and Patrick Nugent, President Johnson's son-in-law (left), share KP duties at Travis Field in Savannah, Georgia, during summer training. (*Chicago Tribune*, July 21, 1966)

LETTERS

16 August 1968
Stockholm

Dear Jim,[12]

Amazingly enough, I did get your letter. I was glad to hear from you; I have wondered about you often. My present situation will take some explaining. I was activated on January 25, just like you. We were due to be sent to Vietnam, but a long political stink arose which involved Pat Nugent.[13] The upshot was that we did not go; Nugent transferred to another unit to get over there, and the Iowa National Guard went instead. I heard that Colorado went shortly thereafter, in March or something. Well, in the middle of May, we were sent to Myrtle Beach, South Carolina, after much confusion, rumors, and counter-rumors all invented to confuse the troops and give the brass something to do, right! Toward the beginning of July, I got word that I was to go to Vietnam. Well, you know me well enough not to be surprised to learn that instead I went to Sweden. I figured that by the end of one-and-a-half years, I could have learned Swedish and started a new life. I like the complete change in landscape. The European mentality suits me well, and I am very fond of the lakes, rocks, brisk air, and blue skies of this country. My wife, Rosemary, came over shortly after I did and likes it as well. She had been here in her junior year in college. At one point, I had decided that I would do the routine, but when I realized that I had an alternative, I took it. I know that in our unit nobody wanted to go, but all did except me. I suppose this was partly because there was no choice for them, really.

By now I guess that you are a seasoned regular, which probably means you are cynical as hell. It's never very good to feel used. You will be that much more prepared to fight when you return to the US. There is much to fight for and

---

12 Jim, a friend from the Denver Air National Guard who attended weapons training with Bruce.

President Johnson's son-in-law.

much to do. For me, I could not see remaking my life when I returned from such degradation, so I renounced my right to ever help the society in which I had a natural and birth-given interest. For you, there is no choice but to emerge and find your way, and perhaps lead others. My thoughts are often with you and my other friends who have become involved in that senseless and insane war.

My sincerest love, Bruce
P.S. I wouldn't advise answering this letter.

August 17, 1968
Stockholm

My Dear Mother,

Your last letter troubled and disturbed me, that you should be nervous and upset about us. I have never felt so healthy and joyous as I have since arriving here. The air is clean, and I have stopped smoking. I am progressing well in yoga and discovering the rhythm of health and life. I am learning that we carry our own becoming within us as a tree becomes from its seed, but our roots are not in the earth (never believe that lie), but in the sky, or in a dimension beyond knowing or utterance, that the world is full of many interlocking chains of causality, that one follows them out of habit or need, that to break the bounds of abstraction takes an act whose essence is faith and whose direction is like an arrow—merely to endure after the gathering leap.

I am sitting in a suburban park before a pond with three vertically shooting water fountains. Before me is a low-story apartment; to my right and behind, clusters of stores. To my left is the subway station and shopping mall. There is an air of rational planning.

[Unsigned]

Bruce, 2008–2009

About this time, I was also beginning to make contacts among other deserters and resisters in Stockholm and getting to know my new country and the layout of Stockholm. I still relied heavily on advice I received from Bert, Vesna, and Rosemary.

There was a loose network of deserters and resisters; word of mouth was the predominant form of communication. Meetings were held. I remember one in particular, with perhaps 60 people attending, the biggest such meeting ever (or since). The organizers and speakers seemed intent on demonizing the position of Sweden in the context of the concerns of those there and attempting to pass motions on behalf of the group assembled for an executive authority to act on their behalf. *To do what?* I thought. My experience to date had been that most attending had different and varying motives that led them to their current situation—that most had benefitted from the Swedish government policy on Vietnam and owed their sanctuary to that policy. If anything, the government was to be congratulated and supported in its efforts, and I said so.

In essence, the chairperson said, "Not so." The ensuing spontaneous debate that erupted among those attending led to a temporary adjournment of proceedings for 15 minutes. People needed to pee or take off, as their situations dictated.

There were hastily arranged meetings of like-minded people in small groups in the corners of the room, in the adjoining hallway and stairwells. "The executive committee" adjourned to a secret chamber adjoining the podium. I was a center of attention for what I had said. A young man remarked to me, "You know these guys are financed through the Communist International." Others chimed in with, "They're just a bunch of Trotskyites." My conclusion was that the meeting was a fuckup. There was no other way to describe it. Deserters and resisters in Sweden had become a nexus for international political intrigue at the operant level. The meeting was finally reconvened with half the original people still there. Some motions were passed for further study and limp action.

I was disillusioned with deserter/resister politics and preferred the company of Rosemary's friends: Bert, Vesna, those from the Stockholm International Peace Research Institute (SIPRI) where

Rosemary worked, and associated networks. I would continue to meet people in the network and befriend those who needed someone to tell their story to. Their stories were many.

Most of the resisters were against all aggressive wars in general and against the American aggression in Vietnam in particular. Most also considered it a crime for a technologically developed country to be engaged in the murder of civilians and to be destroying a small, developing, agricultural country.

Among the most publicly prominent American soldiers to arrive in Sweden were four seamen, absent without leave from the aircraft carrier *Intrepid*. I learned that they first met each other on the flight deck, while on station in the Gulf of Tonkin in September 1967. (Disinformation suggested that they were all members of a motor-cycle gang in Norfolk, Virginia, who got drunk one night and all enlisted the following morning.) They wondered among themselves at the wisdom of catapulting multi-million-dollar aircraft laden with bombs, rockets, and napalm against rice farmers. (Disinformation suggested that they "screwed up" on the flight deck and pulled duty in the kitchen, peeling potatoes.) They were on shore leave in October 1967, when they decided to take a train to Tokyo. Looking for some fun, they went to a nightclub and met some *Beheiren*—the Japanese Peace for Vietnam Committee. They talked. The women were nice. They went to their apartment and spent the night, and more nights. How to get out of Japan was the question. They were due back on ship. If they came to the attention of Japanese authorities, they would be taken into custody and returned to US authorities under the status of forces agreement between the United States and Japan. (Later they heard stories about how the *Beheiren* had been infiltrated by Japanese secret police, but their story came before this.) Americans were conspicuous, and they were not to go outside together. Their hosts decided to move them to the countryside where it would be easier to live underground. "Arrangements need to be made," the *Beheiren* said.

Finally, the waiting was over, and in a windowless van, they were driven west to a port town, arrived at night at a darkened dock, and scurried up a freighter gangplank. The crew were speaking what they thought was Russian. Silently, they were shown to a nice stateroom and locked inside with two unarmed guards at the door. "Do not try to leave," one of the guards said in good English.

The ship disembarked before sunrise into a murky, rainy winter night. "This isn't so bad," they said as they surveyed the stateroom appointments. Tired from the sleepless night on the road, they fell asleep. They were shaken awake by four men, dressed in black, carrying AK-47s. "Come with us," the men said. Grabbing for their few belongings, they were told to leave them, were frisked and herded out the door, headed down dark passageways toward the bow.

"Where are we going?" they asked.

"Vladivostok," was the only answer. They learned later that once they had entered international waters, they became interned by the Russian crew.

The AK-47s pointed them into a small compartment near the front of the ship, empty except for a lone light bulb far overhead. The door was closed and securely bolted with the click of a lock sealing their chamber. The seas were heavy with a northwest gale and the compartment went up and down like a roller coaster throughout the day. They told us (while we listened in rapt attention) that they lost track of time and began to feel fear for their fate, for their lives, and even for their sanity.

Finally, they sensed vibrations through the hull which told them they were in calmer waters, and the ship docked. The door was opened and the dark-suited AK-47s waved them out, upstairs, onto a dark, rainy deck, down a gangplank, and into a waiting limousine. Other guards were inside.

"Where are we going?" they asked.

"Would you like some vodka?" was the reply. An airport was nearby, and they were again ushered up stairs and into a big jet. In the air and ravenous after the grueling trip, they were offered food. They slept and one of them remembered landing and refueling in Novosibirsk. When they landed in Moscow, they were somewhat rested but totally disoriented. They had crossed six time zones.

The Moscow "interviews" were like lengthy interrogations, first separately, covering their life history, their motivations, their connections to groups, the details of knowledge about aircraft-carrier operations. All they knew was how the cables got connected to the nose of the aircraft; how, after one plane was catapulted off, the cable was guided into the nose of another aircraft. Interviews were conducted by experts, or so they later surmised by their English fluency, focus, and thoroughness. Probing was especially noticeable when it came to technical details or tactical fleet operations.

Later they met as a group and began to "practice" for the press conference. As the days passed, they relaxed and were treated well—nice rooms, good food, the odd bit of entertainment, but not allowed to wander alone in the outskirts of the city.

The press conference made international headlines: from Moscow, four deserters tell the world of the injustice of the war in Vietnam and their resistance to it. The propaganda machine that had been wound up inevitably slowed down. When it did, an arrangement was made: they were each given some thousands in gold and put on a plane to Stockholm.

By the time I arrived in Stockholm in July 1968, the honeymoon was over for these four seamen. Journalists from the United States no longer wanted to take them to dinner at fancy restaurants.

They were trying to move on with their lives. Some had Swedish girlfriends and worked as casual laborers, sometimes on the docks, sometimes elsewhere.

And many more were the stories. Some said that the smart ones, and there were some, moved out of Stockholm, got jobs in other industrial cities, making Volvos and Saabs, even Bofors canons.[14] Most went with their instincts: a girlfriend, family connections, a job, security, predictability, peace in my time. And for many there was a continuing inner struggle, to reach peace with themselves, to study war no more.

"Lest we forget" became a kind of private joke: the problem was that there wasn't a single day of the year when they could forget. A court martial would conclude that they had abandoned their fellow warriors, disgraced their oath, run in the face of fire. They knew better. But there were always others' judgments to consider, those of society, community, family, and friends. This nagged at their intellect, complicated their lives, led to countless agonies over what had been lost: the lives and limbs of fellow soldiers, alienated parents, brothers, sisters, property, and roots—that sense of place and belonging, of

---

14   A 40 mm, multipurpose cannon manufactured in Sweden.

sequence and sense of life so much taken for granted by so many. Perhaps worst of all was the loss of country, of an America that was just, free, and tolerant, an America one could believe in and die for. To be alienated from so much that was familiar, the physical symptoms sometimes showing up much later as delayed post-traumatic stress disorder. It has been said that no American escaped the repercussions of the 1960s.

It was never clear how many American servicemen were in Sweden. Swedish sources suggest up to 850, a small amount compared to Canada.

Through the network, I learned that I should not travel where US status of forces agreements existed with the UK, Germany, Greece, and even possibly Italy—in Europe this left France, Switzerland, Yugoslavia, Austria, Norway, and Denmark as safe. "Iron curtain" countries were not to be trusted—but India was OK.

LETTERS

Autumn, 1968
Stockholm

Dear Eric,[15]

I remember especially the clear nights with the moon hanging away from the black backdrop and the pin-pointed stars swirling motionlessly. I was much younger then, but I knew the import of discovering such a big sky: it shut my mouth. We would stand on the spine of a rising ridge in the ponderosa and mule deer country of northeast New Mexico and look north to the snow-capped Sangre de Cristo Mountains. Later, I learned of the pueblos and Comanche; the *conquistadors* with their land grants and the *gringos* with their idle dreams. As if anyone could possess such mountains!

---

15 This letter, from Bruce to Rosemary's brother, Eric, refers to New Mexico where Bruce spent a summer during high school at the Philmont Scout Ranch with the Boy Scouts. Eric lived in Santa Fe, NM, not far from there.

I think the Indians knew, and for that they are corralled (a Spanish word); theirs was a dangerous and subversive belief, so eternal. There is little danger; the blood of Christ and the emptiness of the sky hold Midwestern schoolboys and Swedish dropouts to their own promises. Like a member of the family, I cannot question such a marriage; I am learning to listen, however, and the news growing out of all that suffering is not welcome.

. . . I am about to reenter the academic mainstream. On neutral soil perhaps, I can take the plunge without water-wings. I wake each morning and wonder who our masters are today, but somehow, they never seem to change; or are always changing but acting the same anyway. We were deeply flattered by your long letter and somewhat apprehensive over your first steps [concerning Eric's resistance to the draft]. The rebel can live only in his own sanity. Whatever that necessitates, he must do, always being careful not to overdo.

Bruce

September 23, 1968
Sollentuna[16]

Dear Folks,

. . . I have entered the preliminary take-off stage with my Swedish. Both of us are applying at the university which is, naturally, free, and are trying to determine the possibilities there. I am beginning to understand more and more what is going on around me, which is good, although I haven't quite invented a cover story that I'm completely satisfied with . . .

Rosemary cooked a good chicken and rice dish with salad. She does very well for only one burner! Fall started here in the second week of September. We are wearing

16   A suburb of Stockholm.

sweaters and jackets during the day. I can't wait for the winter! I have been seeing a little of Parker S. We ran around together the summer of 1961 and saw each other sporadically thereafter. He deserted in February. Rosemary has been running into several old acquaintances at her new job and is busily sending out resumes. I am staying busy. I have taken up your suggestion, Mom, and am writing a little, although it is still sporadic and unsure. My yoga is progressing well; it is a very important part of my life now and I may well teach it professionally some day. I am coming to increasingly distrust the workings of pure abstraction; I see so much perversion of purpose and stifling of will under the guise of objectivity in the States! But I am more sad than angry when I think of the US and the election, and the police (Bob W. made an incorrect turn in his car; the police stopped him; he is now recovering with 14 stitches in his head and a charge for assaulting an officer), and the war (Peter H. really seems determined to come to Sweden next year). I keep firing off letters to people in the hope that some will be reminded; it is so difficult when one is in the middle of it. If I could legally return to the US tomorrow, I doubt that I would; and if I did, it would be to become a political activist. The United States needs a revolution and may get one even if she doesn't [need it]. The Social Democrats won handily in the election here, showing that the "swing to the right in Europe" was not one of the laws of nature. I think that you would like Sweden; it has restored my faith in man to see a nation behave so rationally, but there are reasons: she is caught between [nations] and is highly circumspect. This explains her foreign policy, but not her domestic policy which is the thing that impresses me more, for the very reason that it is a voluntary association, a willed humanitarianism.

Bruce

Today[17]
Sollentuna

Dear Folks,

. . . Finances here are quite insane. People get on a list for housing through a co-op arrangement, pay a down payment, and rent for the rest of their lives! They have legal exclusive use, but do not own. Ownership is felt to be a primitive instinct anyway! (I really like it, theoretically.)

Rosemary just got a full-time job making $400 a month which puts us in the 40% income tax bracket. About magazines: the Wolfs[18] are getting us the *International Newsweek*, but if you want to make us a present of six months of the *International Herald Tribune*, you can deposit 117 kroner into our account (that's about $23). It is printed daily in Paris and carries all the important international and domestic news (US news). Through it, we have followed the campaigns, the interesting court action against the 1966 law which was used to call up the reserves. (If it's unconstitutional, it will very directly affect me.) We have been getting it copy by copy at the newsstand cost of $0.30 . . . (Aaaahem) Rosemary and I (mostly Rosemary) are earning a little extra money by typing a guy's memoirs. An old Swedish doctor; he's doing it in English, so everybody can read them! He is very corny. Since when are memoirs a series of bad jokes; and in English? Phew! It pays good anyway, $1.00 a page for triple-spaced typing. I think that the old guy will find that no publisher will touch them. The dreams of immortality. Which reminds me, I started yoga classes once a week.

Your loving son, Bruce

---

17 October 4, 1968.
18 Rosemary's parents.

19 November 1968

Dearest Mark,[19]

I feel terribly guilty about not writing to you before this, so I'm trying to get off my note here at work. Hoping no one comes in and catches me. And of course, it will take ages to reach you, since I will send it via my parents [the Wolfs]. We had a note from Bob, saying the FBI had been to visit you again. God, what a bloody pain—do you think you will have to move? We've been involved with enough deserters, etc., now to know that if they wanted to find us here in Stockholm, I'm sure they could. They just delight in hassling folk—and I'm terribly sorry you got the wrong end of the stick . . .

. . . We have moved. We now live in the very center of Stockholm in the old part of town—narrow streets, artsy shops, etc. Sort of the Georgetown of Stockholm. We got our apartment through a friend, and we were very lucky to get it. We have one room and a kitchen in an old house with terribly high ceilings and enormous windows overlooking the courtyard of a large church across the road. It's not completely modern, but we have hot water through a gadget on the kitchen wall, a stove, a refrigerator, a toilet, and one electric radiator. We also have a tile oven, for which we order wood every week. The church across the street has a public bath and swimming pool which we can use.

We went through a bit of a crisis two or three weeks ago. You see, our work permits and residence permits are only issued for three months at a time, and apparently just about everyone whose permits had expired was not getting them renewed. They were waiting anywhere from one to four or five months and getting nowhere. Finally, there was a big piece in the papers when a whole group of Americans were

---

19   From Rosemary to Mark German, the previously mentioned soldier from Panama who was nearly killed in the 1964 Panamanian riots. Mark sublet Bruce and Rosemary's apartment in Washington, DC, and cared for their cat, Raj.

here to visit (representatives of several left-wing groups plus clergy men who were visiting deserters here and in France, making propaganda here, and supposedly preparing a report to be released prior to the US election thereby influencing it in some way—I can't see where anything happened), and the interior minister said that the Swedish policy had not changed, no one was going to kick us out, etc., and about a week later everyone got their permits renewed . . .

Bruce got a job, the better to preserve his work permit when it did run out. We were lucky, and a Yugoslavian friend, a chemist, got him a job in her factory, though he is in the packing department, putting inventory into cartons for delivery prior to the Christmas rush. Really shitty, and he starts at 6:45 in the morning, so must get up at 5:30 which is hell. Fortunately, the job is just a few station rides on the subway without changing. I guess he will remain there till Christmas, if he can take it that long and perhaps then work at something else—depending on what he can find—or else begin school. He has been accepted at the university, so it is just a matter of registering, and beginning to work on the first *betyg*, or series of courses. Most of the work is private reading and research. But the system is such that we have to choose between going on for a PhD in our chosen field and starting over again to get a *Fil. Kand*, which is a little more advanced than a BA, but it is like starting college over. So that is rather a discouraging prospect . . .

Anyway, along with all the tension and turmoil about work and residence permits, Bruce and I decided to get involved with some of the other deserters in forming a new group for "self-help and liaison with the Swedish community." The old group—the ADC [American Deserter Committee]—presently consists of about four deserters and six speed freaks; it is elitist and has been playing personality games with members of the Swedish Vietnam Committee, the PNL group, Swedish Maoists, etc., and has been accusing anyone half sensible of being a CIA agent. Over the last few months the ADC had alienated any of the support which the group had. So, we tried to form a new group, got a bit enthusiastic over the possibilities, met some very nice Swedes, and even some interesting Americans. However, it soon became apparent that the deserters were not terribly interested in what we considered the primary thing, i.e., adjustment to Swedish life, but were mostly interested in playing left-wing political games. Bruce calls them a "phantastic group of dreamers and would-be Lenins" and I think that description is quite apt. After we had gotten things off to a rather sensible start, the movement got bogged down by a French Buddha who introduced concepts of rotational democracy, sensitivity groups for contemplation, the unities, and all sorts of other groovy things and I have stopped going to the meetings . . .

Rosemary

December 4, 1968

Dear Mark,

We hear from Ella Mae that you had a visitor.[20] Ella Mae said that the story broke in the Oklahoma City and Norman papers on August 3rd. I still haven't been officially notified but expect to be on Monday; they told me to be there [in Myrtle Beach] in the morning. I'm taking six hours of Swedish a day and awaiting developments. Will probably have more news by next week. I wanted to make a special point of thanking you; it was a big help to Rosemary as she has often mentioned. I was glad that someone was there to help her, and especially glad that it was a friend. If you were serious about quitting the U. S., we could line up a job for you here. It is necessary to have one *before* coming to Sweden to get a work permit. I have found the country to be rational in the extreme. To the American disaffected liberal, this comes

---

20 Mark was visited and questioned many times by the FBI when he lived in Bruce and Rosemary's old apartment.

as a great shock, for his opinions are state policy. There is no necessity for a defensive stance; no agony of guilt; no unrequited yearnings of that sort. There are problems, but their nature is completely different, e.g., see Ingmar Bergman. More again soon. Let us hear from you.

Your friend, Bruce

Bruce, 2008–2009

There must have been some connection between Mark German and Panama that kept bringing the FBI back to Mark's door. It couldn't simply be that Mark had taken over our apartment, being better than the one he had. Mark had been in the army, stationed in the Canal Zone, listening to radio traffic, classified as to frequencies, purpose, and results, about the same time that I was there for Christmas, 1962, visiting my parents and the rest of my sibs, A, C, and D.

Ella Mae posed for Mark's wife [the painter, Elaine German]. I only met him later, as a friend of the family. But, I had written a paper for a postgraduate seminar in "problem-solving," something related to US diplomacy. The professor was an ex-employee of the diplomatic service or something, but still had connections to the Service. He may have submitted my paper to them. The paper, like the *Pelican Brief*, posited that if the Panamanian government was arguing that they were being ripped off by the United States, which was gaining lots of revenue from tolls through the Panama Canal, the United States should open the books to the Panamanians, show them the huge costs in maintaining the canal, and the cost-neutral nature of the whole undertaking. In this way, a joint partnership agreement could be reached, with the Government of Panama an equal partner in the canal endeavor. It was in both their interests to maintain a peaceful traffic flow through the canal. This was the position that the United States adopted—with the benefit of my paper or not.

In Stockholm in the fall of 1968, I received a message that someone wanted to talk to me. I called them. They wanted to meet at an address in Ostermalm. I went. Strange setup, first floor suite, peace buttons on display: "Are you familiar with this symbol?" Yeah, so what, why am I here? "Do you know anybody in Panama?" Sure, been there. More probing, more non-committal responses.

LETTERS

December 9, 1968

Dear Mark,

With some sense of resignation mingled strongly with excitement and suppressed hope, I am venturing back onto the academic road. At the ripe age of 25, I realize that political science is the only thing I can really take a personal and lasting interest in; the only thing I really know anything about! Strange, since I'm personally becoming more and more apolitical. My fellow deserters . . . I'm afraid I have less respect for than my friends who had to go through the agony of doubt to go, and went, and will return knowing that all of it was a big game. My fellow deserters do not know this, and their superegos feed the death wish at very high energy levels. So back to academia; perhaps the game can be made more humane; perhaps people will yet learn to laugh at themselves.

No, the hardships and uncertainties don't really amount to much. They leave you with a clear head; somewhat sad, but sadness without tension, without fatigue. Do you remember Peter H., the one in Japan? He wrote from his experience and advised me to practice the sense of "disembodied consciousness," which used to be taken up with the serio-comic games with friends, familiar environments, etc.

We'll be glad to get *Newsweek* for the sciences, art, etc. (politics—ho hum). I'm reading Marcuse if that helps in interpreting what I'm saying. In my own vague way, I am building a concept of politics based on Marx, Freud, Einstein, Yoga, Zen and Charlie Brown. It's not easy. I read that the Yippies "played to the cameras" and I'm wondering when the media is going to get smart and pull a coup in Washington (really!). About cigarettes: as you know it's an oral habit. I think it took Yoga to get me to quit, with no hang-ups. Maybe it could be done painlessly in another way. My advice is don't bother unless you're indifferent to the whole karma; otherwise your mind will compensate and probably in a destructive way. The deserters mostly have identity problems. You know how even cosmopolitan, educated Americans hang together abroad? These guys have a stronger propensity. Most have high school or less; no foreign exposure. Some have adjusted; you don't hear from them or about them; this may be a large majority. I just don't know. The others are playing a basically destructive cliquish revolutionary game with the CIA (their fantasy).

With all those flicks and plays, you're doing much more than we are, but I can empathize with the sense of fatigue with surroundings and friends. I think that's probably a good deal of what was behind my decision, which I still don't understand. A good move is always pretext for getting rid of junk and culling connections so long as it fits into some longer-range, very personal way of interpreting one's presence here . . . We are existential by virtue of habit, by virtue of cliché, by virtue of virtue! Back to poetry. Before I go into complete babble, I must say goodbye. Love to Raj, Bob, and Doris, and the shit machine. If my letters in the future are all theory, forgive me but I cannot say what I will directly; for perhaps we can only eat the same food.

Bruce

Bruce, 2008–2009

I got another call; phoned back and went to the address given to me. I was picked up by a guy in a new Volvo who parked a half block down from the American Deserters Committee (ADC) headquarters. The driver said, "Watch this" as a figure emerged from the ADC building, jumped into a car at the curb, started the engine, ground the gears into first, and pulled away in a cloud of engine exhaust. "You see," my driver said, "burned out on amphetamines." I never knew who the Volvo driver was or where he came from. Judging from the origin of the call, however, I have concluded he was a Swedish internal security operative, on a mission to dissuade me from affiliation with the ADC.

LETTERS

December 9, 1968
Sollentuna

Dear Folks,

I feel much more settled now after that initial shock caused by such a violent change. You'd be surprised what getting on a plane, going you're not sure where will do to one's head. At the same time, many cobwebs seem to have been cleared away and the non-emotive clarity of an existential awareness I find very comfortable because it weighs absolutely nothing . . .

Love, Bruce

7 January 1969

Dear Mark,[21]

---

21   From Rosemary.

As for the poor American, may I say that the Vietnam War has done a very thorough job of making all Americans appear to be in introverted, weak-minded, aggressive, and cruel. Even the attempts to stop the war through protest and political action appear as too little, too late. So that, it seems to me here, people have ceased to feel that Americans can do any decent intellectual work. That is, they think all Americans are too blind and deceived by their government to be able to make any contribution to the general knowledge and working of a peaceful international atmosphere and reality. Does that make sense? Being on this end, I feel rather bitter about that aspect and think in many ways it will be one of the sad results of the war . . . that American intellectual effort comes to be less respected.

Bruce's response to the news of Raj's alteration [being spayed] was: "Poor Raj, only one Maoist offspring." Actually, we sympathize with your decision. Knowing her general personality and having seen her in heat twice, I know that Raj is too much of a spoiled princess to keep her ill temper to herself . . .

Love, Rosemary

P.S. They probably read our letters at the post office . . . maybe you shouldn't save them.

Chapter Three

Winterfunk

LETTERS

February 11, 1969
Gamla stan

Why I Deserted

The reasoning was remarkably clear, the path was open, and the need fed upon the logic of the situation. From the summer of 1965 to the summer of 1968, I was employed by one branch or another of the Department of Defense, first as an intelligence analyst trainee that graduated into order of battle studies in Latin America, and then as an aerial-photographic interpreter. It was largely because of this last assignment that I came into contact with North Vietnam. It is a pleasant-looking little backwater along the coast of the South China Sea. As I inspected this gracefully sweeping arc of beach and patchwork of rice paddies behind, I often pondered the threat of this peasant kingdom to the security of the United States. The servants of my detached viewing were the pilots and equipment of the navy and air force: sleek F-101s, F-8s, and the honey of both services, the RF-4C. Coming in fast and low over that long beach from their carriers in the Gulf of Tonkin, or through the back door from bases in South Vietnam and, increasingly, Thailand, I could often see peasants flat on their stomachs in vegetable fields or caught in a crouch by the fast-moving panoramic cameras. The roads, but especially the road and rail approaches to bridges, were badly chewed up by the spring of 1967 when I was viewing a sizeable portion of the aerial photography shot over southern Vietnam. It was obvious that perhaps considerable numbers of civilians were being killed, and I could understand personally the charges about a "credibility gap" then just beginning to be aired. When an opportune truck park was assembled in a small town, the civilians were especially vulnerable. I knew too well that this effort to cut the supply routes to the south was not having a measurable effect on the level of conflict in South Vietnam, to say nothing of the taxpayer cost for over a thousand multi-million-dollar aircraft and perhaps twice as many airmen. Militarily then, the bombing was an ill-conceived strategy. This much is history.

As my understanding of the military establishment began to gain breadth, I realized that I was in a particularly advantageous position to study it. I was in the intelligence section of the Joint Chiefs of Staff, those men from the Pentagon whose advice and counsel in world affairs was to gain more and more influence in the 1960s, until they embroiled the US in progressive apoplexy. It was a business with which I wanted nothing to do, and I made plans to withdraw as a civilian and pursue teaching where I thought my vision of a more worthwhile world could be appropriately applied. This brief interruption in my three years with the military suddenly ended on the day in late January 1968 when the president activated airmen and soldiers of the nation's National Guard following the Pueblo incident. Finally, in the summer of 1968, when I received orders to go to Vietnam, I realized that all my stratagems to avoid becoming involved in this dirtiest of senseless wars had failed. The only remaining decision was whether to continue in the path of error.

These points of decision in one's life can pass with such little notice, almost as if they represented some form of fate. So, I came to Sweden and have been attempting to rebuild my life, a refugee of the Vietnamese War. Perhaps only time, considerable time, will ever allow me to return to the country of my birth and love, to the familiar places, friends, and family. It was a sacrifice that I willingly accepted, knowing that the last amnesty in the US was after the Civil War, that it might take a very long time for Americans to forget that they are not always right. It is one thing to admit privately, quite another to advocate it publically, much less politically.

[Unsigned]

Bruce, 2008-2009

Rosemary, having spent her university junior year abroad in Stockholm, had already mastered basic Swedish. She had also met some influential people and was referred to the Stockholm International Peace Research Institute (SIPRI) where she applied successfully to be an editor of their publications. Their working language was English and staff members were normally seconded from a variety of countries, including Great Britain, Yugoslavia, and Germany. Along with Bert and Vesna, these people were the focus of our social life.

In a suburb of Stockholm, close to an above-ground subway station, there was a chemical plant run by a cooperative, bought from a German firm. They made laundry and dish detergents, shampoo, and soap and experimented with a limited line of cosmetics. Our friend Vesna had arranged a job for me in the warehouse, filling orders from cooperative stores in towns throughout Sweden. I would push a large cart up and down the wide aisles of the windowless cavern, reading from the printed order and pick the items off the shelves, stack them on the cart and, when finished, return to the control desk and load the order onto a pallet, to be picked up by a forklift for delivery to the railroad or truck dock.

I started work in November of 1968, my first job following language training. They needed extra help for the retail build-up to Christmas. I rode the subway to work in the dark crowded among other workers. Usually, 20–30 workers would emerge through the sliding doors at the factory's stop, an eight-minute walk away from the beginning of their shift. There was some conversation among workers, but most were silent in their plodding, dressed in casual clothes, wearing their synthetic wool hats and carrying briefcases. The briefcases contained their lunch. Management usually drove to work and wore genuine fur hats. You had to look closely at first to tell the managers and professionals from the workers, but soon the status differences became apparent despite all the efforts to smudge them. A locker room was provided for changing into work clothes. I always felt alone—my Swedish was still rudimentary and definitely not adequate for the jocularity and repartee of my male coworkers, particularly at the end of the day when everybody was in a better mood, looking forward to their evening and perhaps some diversion or their happy hour. They might be headed for the state liquor store, briefcase in hand, to disguise their purchase while they walked the last stretch home under neighbors' eyes. I lingered at my locker and often used the shower rooms provided. Our apartment did not have a shower. The walk back to the subway station for the trip home was also in the dark. This was the flip side of those wonderfully long sunny days in July and August.

My fellow workers in the warehouse were not particularly friendly, simply because communicating with me was cumbersome and I had to ask a lot of questions at first about what something on the list meant and where it was located. The other temporary worker hired for the Christmas rush caught on much quicker and my questions seemed to be resented, as if he was wasting his time and I was slow to comprehend. I noticed that I was given shorter order lists than others, from the cooperative stores in small towns, often up north. I finally understood this when, close to the time for my temporary job to end after Christmas, a coworker was happy and excited, exclaiming to all that, "I have a contract." I asked myself, *what does this mean?*

I did not understand the answer, but Vesna explained it to me that night. Her English was good, and the answer was that a "contract" is an agreement with an employer that relates "productivity" to pay. The more soap you put on your pallet in a given period, the more you get paid. Now I understood why my coworker had gotten so friendly with the supervisor who passed out the order lists.

I had never had a job or remembered a school day in my life that started in the dark and ended in the dark, much less occurred in a building with no windows, only the hum of fluorescent lights. At lunchtime, I had gotten into the habit of climbing the stairwell of the adjoining building to gaze south through its big windows to see the sun, low on the horizon.

These were the only times besides the weekends that I saw the sun for seven weeks. Shortly after Christmas, I was laid off. I was relieved. Although unemployed and uncertain about my prospects, I no longer felt like an automaton. I had saved enough to buy a cheap stereo system and borrowed records from friends. Music had been important to me and now I could enjoy it again.

Our apartment in Gamla stan ["old town"], however, was unheated, cold, and damp. I borrowed a handsaw and an old piece of luggage from Bert and discovered various building and renovation sites within walking distance where I would rummage through the construction waste in search of wood. Much of the wood had been used to make concrete forms and I discovered that when it was burned, it would pop loudly, sending sparks into the apartment if the wire cover was not in front of the tile oven that occupied the corner of our one room. There was a kitchen, long and narrow. It had a sink, a two-burner stove that required a token to start the gas flowing, and a small electric water heater above the sink. A tiny adjacent room held a toilet. Electricity was expensive, so we only turned on the water heater shortly before we needed it to wash in morning, or to clean up from supper. We had to plan ahead to make sure that we had enough tokens to prepare a meal, especially since the local kiosk that sold them closed early.

Gathering wood was my biggest chore since it had to be carried 20 pounds at a time in the luggage. At first, I rather enjoyed this task. It gave me an excuse to get outside and explore the meandering medieval streets. At least I was doing something to improve our situation; I had the time and there was no cost in the effort. After the first week, however, the available construction sites were farther away; those close by had been exhausted or the work completed. As well, the longer planks had to be sawed into smaller pieces to be carried. If I had enough wood, I didn't mind having to get up in the middle of the night to keep the fire going. At least we could stay warm. I was often reminded of a scene from an Ibsen play, where a turn-of-the-century poor Stockholm poet was obsessed with the plastering and taping of cracks in his apartment's windows and walls, vainly fighting off the cold and damp drafts. The poet was depressed to be too poor to burn more than one candle at a time, and certainly could not afford firewood.

It was here, on Västerlånggatan, in the unheated second floor walk-up, that we spent our first Christmas in Sweden. Lying in bed by the window, we could look up and see the steeple of the Tyska Kyrka (German church) in the Old Town. Lucia, the celebration of the returning of the light on December 21, was a hopeful sign, even if the worst weather was yet to follow. Rosemary even went to the trouble of adorning herself with a wreath of lingonberry twigs with four candles burning and bringing me saffron buns in bed with coffee, as was the custom. Christmas coincided with older Yule and winter festivals of the Vikings, and the Christian aspect of the holidays was more muted than in North America. For us, this was the first Christmas away from contact with any of our family. It was a time when Swedish friends would invite us to their modern apartments and we would take a towel to enjoy the luxury of friends' showers. The apartment in the Old Town did not have bathing facilities and the nearest public bath was open to men only on alternate days, two days a week—women had the other two days when it was open. At our friends', there was good food and wine and some singing. Central heating was great on these occasions.

Winter, 1968. Bruce contemplates the Christmas tree in their tiny apartment.

Vesna was a Yugoslavian woman, trained as a chemist. She immigrated to Sweden some years before, after meeting Bert on a Mediterranean beach. She wore one of those macramé net bikinis that were popular in the 1960s. Bert told her about the good life in Sweden and helped her with the immigration. That was years before and it was difficult to say what their relationship was now. Clearly, they were friends.

Rosemary, Bert, Vesna, and I would often go cross-country skiing together at one of the many parks or greenbelts and end up at Bert's 12th floor apartment in Nacka for showers, a change of clothes, some wine, conversation, cooking, and hands of hearts. Occasionally we would dine out or go to a movie together.

In the soap and cosmetics factory, Vesna would analyze competitors' products and suggest new concoctions. Bert was a senior civil servant, judging by his bachelorhood, Volvo, apartment, and sailboat. He never talked about his work but had lots of interests and liked the outdoors.

From Bert's apartment, you could look out large windows over a landscape of other high-rise apartments, widely spaced so there were vistas between them, over a *torp* (bald granite hilltop) to the main channel into Stockholm harbor.

Rosemary and I met many others, too: the Americans in the underground network, friends of friends. Some of my fellow war resisters weren't so fortunate, working the docks, washing dishes, and holding down various jobs.

LETTERS

February 18, 1969
Gamla stan

Dear Folks,[22]

. . . It's slowly getting lighter, but the weather has turned colder. We must build a fire in the fireplace almost every day now to supplement the heat of our electric radiator. (Last week several days were -11 degrees F.) . . . Regarding Mom's last letter. Yes, I know how to ski; I learned in New Hampshire in my sophomore year, also skied several times in Denver when I was there in 1967. Have never had lessons. It's not hard. Many men in their 70s and 80s ski regularly during the season. Re: yoga—I'm still doing yoga, taking instruction from Karin Schallander at The Yoga Institute

---

22 This letter was written on February 18, 1969, and finally sent in August of 1970 with this addendum: "Now let's all admit that we have soldiers in the house."

here; it is supposed to be one of the very best in Europe. She is a beautiful blonde. I stand on my head five minutes every day. Some of the other postures are indescribable.

My courses—in the morning we study Swedish in Swedish; in the afternoon we study international relations and political science in English; next year it will all be in Swedish.

Rosemary here: I'm working on two projects. One is an annual report on armament and disarmament, progress reports in both, including defense expenditures, technological developments, nil progress in disarmament, etc. The other has to do with weapons trade with the third world, developing countries. My work is on the research side, but more like a librarian. Too complicated to explain.

Goodbye for now. This letter (if you hadn't guessed) was a community project, dictated by Bruce, typed and edited by Rosemary. Bruce is doing the ironing.

Love, B & R

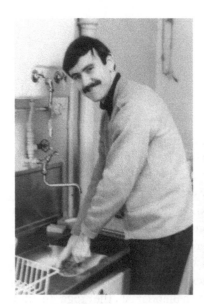 

LEFT: Bruce washes dishes in their apartment in Gamla stan.
RIGHT: Rosemary warms herself at their fireplace.

March 11, 1969[23]
Omnia Stan

My concern and interest in the problems of international community date most explicitly from the call that the late President Kennedy made to all of us now in our mid-20s. I shared with so many the loss which seems more than ever now to have been a spiritual loss to the country. With the majority, I voted with Johnson to end the war in '64. It was the first and last general election in which I voted, a poor record of meaning in such turbulent times. Although the country seemed to be convinced that it was merely a matter of the lesser of two evils in the fall of '68, the spirit had largely gone out of the campaign before the Republicans met in Miami. Subsequent events only served to nauseate those who had been so close to events for so long and seemed to awaken those who had thought it sufficient to ignore the growing barbarization and authoritarianism of American civilization. Now that the mask of inactivity has been torn from the image of the administration, the American people seem to be at least awakening to the realization that they no longer are leaders of their own destiny. Strange counsel is being made in secret corridors of the Pentagon. The president is more isolated from the public than ever, and widely supported demonstrations of public opinion somehow fall outside the legitimate range of political expression. America is now in the grips of a colossal reexamination of her soul being conducted by every citizen; and I can assure you from the bottom of my understanding, American heart, that the America of his dreams is not in the circles of hell. In the process, the rest of the world is hoping that America learns something of the nature of toleration which is the essence of the human community.

---

23   Although Bruce is the author, the recipient of this letter/essay is unknown.

We cannot, of course, let the platitudes of universality delude us from the reality of conflict. That such conflict can be a creative process[24]

[Unsigned and unfinished]

April 18, 1969

Dearest Mark,

. . . Actually, one reason 1 haven't written is that Bruce and I have been in a pretty down period—the winter has now lasted for six-and-a-half months. First, I had a stiff neck, and now I have a bad stomach thing—which is nerves and tension from work, and maybe, though I doubt it, an ulcer. Bruce is sick of school, feels it's a waste, futile, meaningless. Together, we're a sad pair. Our American friends are getting ready to split, and most of the Swedes have gone to hell.

R

---

24 My brother, having started his academic career again, probably wrote this for a class. Its abrupt abandonment is telling. Perhaps he was wrestling with the validity of the last, unfinished sentence.

Chapter Four
Notes on the Revolution

LETTERS

May 17, 1969
Gamla stan

Dear Alan,

. . . When (within a week) will you be in Stockholm? We are ready for you with an extra mattress, and if I can get together some quick cash, I may join you on the road here to Scandinavia, or later in France. The tulips are just coming up. Don't venture hitchhiking without: 1) a warm sweater, 2) a good raincoat or poncho. Caution: Swedes are known for their coolness; ignore and proceed slowly and sincerely and they will share anything with you. Note: you can camp anywhere but in people's back or front yards. They have a completely different sense of property. Note: most young Swedes speak English and dig speaking it and meeting you. When you get near Stockholm, ask for Gamla stan—then find us; we live one floor up from ground level. Look for the pot plant growing in the window. If the front door is locked, throw pebbles. If open, name is on door. Of course, call. Hear soon, let on, sign off, one voice.

Bruce

19 May 1969

Dear Mark,

. . . Most of the trees are that pale budding green, and the tulips are trying to make it. Looks like Washington in late March. I've stopped reading everything except letters, poetry, and rarely, fiction. I think that I just ran out of space for concepts and abstractions. Visions still interest me, whether of the poetic type or the flashes of memory and ironic juxtaposition of mood. I can see out that window[25] which the sun streams through in the late afternoon, so Raj can take it in and see America happening in the alleyway. I thought that I could study America through that window and saw that there were many people to be. We have shared lots of those ghost images that some call roles. Somewhere, the logic that impelled me toward teaching has taken me to heart, and I have found that to accept life without reflection. I know that [preceding line] is no sentence, but a revolutionary will stop at nothing(!)

. . . I've also been learning some things about sewing. It's lousy and it'll ruin your eyes. Seamstresses are the most underpaid people in the world! I've had so much free time that I've just been keeping house, and that doesn't keep me busy. Now I know why women crochet and all that jazz, not to mention drinking those patent medicines for the codeine. Whoever said you need a book to learn? I'm hoping to get a job with the social welfare people. Sweden is very advanced in this field, so I'll withhold a description until I get the job. It sounds interesting and worthwhile to me.

Notes on the revolution: I'm finding more and more of it a little neurotic. That takes some explaining: not the logic, the premises, the ethical standards or the vision of humanity, but the revolutionaries themselves. This is all to say that they make me uncomfortable. I've seen them here looking for power and glory, and when it deceives them, they appear as children on a drill field, wailing against being splashed with

---

25   The west window in Bruce's old Washington, DC, apartment.

mud. The beautiful ones, the ones who are sacrificed, live as immortals for the attempt. They are the true ones, and their moments are rare in history.

On Sunday we went for a walk along the Malaren and stopped for a coffee and cakes at a pavilion by the water. Very pleasant to watch the ducks and sailboats. The winter is so long that one can easily forget that Stockholm is a beautiful city.

Still looking for an apartment . . .

I've been thinking about the quote of Morgenthau's[26] that you sent: viz. "America has only expatriates." To support his point about how other countries have "temporary émigrés," he cites the obvious case from which he borrowed the word, and the returns to Fascist countries of self-exiles. It is interesting to ponder how many people left to stay in cases where they could have returned. I personally know of several such cases and would guess that motivation as to living place is much more deeply disturbed; that life patterns are more irrevocably changed by no alternative more than Morgenthau suggests. I would venture to say that this—exiles and their relationship (attitudinal and spatial) to their native country—defies generalization! That is somewhat heretical I know. However, I do feel that most meaning-structures are imposed and resemble any other product in their currency, circulation, duplication, etc. Abstractions depend on authority for their compatibility and acceptance. Does Morgenthau suggest that the English language has no such word as "émigré?" That's absurd. Does he suggest that the "purpose of American politics" is to synthesize a political continuity which makes "sense" only on the abstract level and is therefore incapable, like logic, of admitting to its own imperfections and thereby changing and growing? If he did that, it would mean he has ventured very far indeed from the Establishment Reality, for he would be admitting that there are cases when individual vision can transcend national purpose. I doubt if Morgenthau is even as revolutionary as

---

26 Hans Morgenthau, 1904–1980, a leading twentieth-century figure in the study of international politics.

Huckleberry Finn. He continues to base his politics on semantic abstractions. My assumption here is simple: a clever person is always at least one step ahead of the best generalization. This leaves "the nature of reality" hanging in mid-air in this metaphysical system. That's where it belongs! To finish this off, let me say that Morgenthau seems to say little except that America doesn't change in order to accept the returned exile. Besides, I knew many "European-crazy" students who, come spring, couldn't wait to get back to the USA. For myself, I would probably return but for the jail term . . .

Bruce

Spring, 1969[27]
Gamla stan

We've been sending tapes like this to Rosemary's folks, and we've learned that no matter how dearly you love someone, making a tape is rather a difficult proposition; it enables one to come across, but it also takes a bit of time consciously set aside for the purpose . . .

You mentioned the insanity over the anti-ballistic missile system. I don't know if you understand the relationship between that and cassette tape recorders, but it is probably one of those technological spin-offs from the missile race, which is kind of ironic, but I suppose we can all just hope that the spin-offs keep going in the right directions. Someone computed recently that if the Russians were to launch their anti-ballistic missiles (which they are supposed to have eventually, of course) at the American missiles (launched at the Soviet Union for any number of reasons) then all the interception would take place right over Sweden, which would

---

27 Transcribed from a cassette tape recording continuously playing background music from Donovan's *Mellow Yellow* album. The tape was addressed to Bruce's brother Dan, and his wife, Judy.

mean that Sweden, the great neutralist non-nuclear power, would be the chief sufferer from the all-out war, which is kind of an interesting reflection.

Your illusions of grandeur, as you call them (I'm talking now from notes I took from your tape, Dan—trying to answer the implicit questions, and comment on some of the things you brought up), about shooting higher than you were already. I suppose what you mean is that you feel you're developing your own style somehow and you want an area to give it adequate expression; that's how I interpreted your remarks. When you said something about not seeing any sense in writing since you're always changing, Dan, I thought of something I had read from Rilke, *The Notebooks of Malte Laurids Brigge*;[28] it's a short two paragraphs, perhaps I should read both of them:

> I am learning to see. I don't know why it is, but every-thing penetrates me more deeply, and does not stop at the place where, until now it always used to finish. I have an inner self of which I was ignorant. Everything goes thither now, what happens there I do not know.

> Writing a letter today, I was struck by the fact that I had been here only three weeks; three weeks elsewhere, in the country, for example, would be like a day. Here it has seemed like years, and I mean to write no more letters. What's the use of telling anyone that I am changing? If I am changing, then surely I am no longer the person I was, and if I am something else than heretofore, then it is clear that I have no acquaintances, and to strange peo-ple, to people who do not know me, I cannot possibly write . . .

And then you mentioned something about a dope addic-tion problem. You remember when it really hit the States? Well, it happened to Sweden this last fall, so there was a lot of hysteria. But interestingly enough, the Netherlands has been taking a very progressive attitude toward it; they have

28 *Stories of God.*

public places where the kids smoke pot. The attempts on the part of society are to integrate the kids, give them a sense of belonging, a sense of whatever it is that motivates a society in a constructive direction. At least they have enough faith in their society to feel that love is an answer.

Spring has finally come to Sweden; it's long overdue in my book. I remember the day back in early September when the cold wind came out of the north. I thought it was unusual, but it was the beginning of winter, and it didn't get warm again. It was the kind of cold you don't get ever in New Haven until late October, perhaps early November. And it really hasn't gotten warm until this week. We had a slight respite over Easter, which was beautiful, but now it's beginning to warm up just a little bit; it snowed for three straight days about a week ago, but that's gone; you still have to wear a coat. I would say in Fahrenheit it's in the upper thirties, lower forties. Sometimes it blows my mind, though: I was sitting out in the square today, and the sun was baking down, and I felt nice and warm with my jacket open, but as I breathed I noticed that my breath was forming little clouds . . . My head is completely spaced-out from sunlight. The days are getting much longer now; it's beginning to wake me up at four in the morning with bright sunlight and doesn't get dark until about 8:30. There's an immediate post sunset—deep, steel-blue the sky has—and I've only seen that before in Denver . . .

. . . It's now several days, a week, I don't know how much later. It's morning, I'm sitting here, just finished my breakfast, sent Rosemary off to work; we had french toast. I'm contemplating what to do today; so far having figured that I would run up to the university to see somebody in the department about the graduate program next year. My desk is completely littered with all kinds of shit from two half-inch-thick term papers, various correspondence, newspapers, clippings people send to me, all sorts of crap that people stop by to leave off, all piled high here on the desk. My studies this semester haven't been particularly pressing. It just occurred to me though how involved you and Judy are in your work; your work is such a substantial part of your life, and with me it seems kind of . . . well, it's pretty hard to say. I've been going through some changes. I don't want to have to sound like I have to justify not working because I really don't think that people must work. I think it's more a matter of mental health, mental balance, than it is income (certainly we aren't pressed in any way as far as income goes), but it's very funny, the different attitude I've taken toward political science since I started back in at the university. As near as I can figure out, the whole field is an immense pile of bullshit. I did a paper, for instance, on militarism in Latin America, which I haven't finished (I did about a 15-page preliminary research note), and, comparing all the source information and some of the hypotheses concerning militarism, all the results have been, more or less, random correlations between things like US economic aid and coups d'état, correlations between the size of the middle classes and the number of coups d'état, all of these correlations are either random, or evidence is conflicting. The point I'm trying to make is that statistically and empirically there's not enough evidence even for a pre-theory, much less a theory of politics. This has coincided with some of my other interpretations of the world that I've been making. The world seems to consist of just very simply, people. And of course, the social sciences are based on the assumption that there is some kind of order underlying society which transcends mere individuality. Vaguely, for instance, that social roles can or do determine behavior. From what I've been able to see so far, it doesn't make any difference. You get good people and bad people, the left-wing movements, the right-wing movements, and the theater movements in the universities and military . . .

One thing I didn't mention: I'm getting deeply involved with yoga. Up until just recently it's been primarily a physical thing. I've known about the mental aspects but approached it as something to be learned physically. My attitude there has changed; one of the primary assumptions of Hindu philosophy is that the phenomenal reality has its own chain of causes and effects, and that the true oneness of the universality of

God, that Godhead within us, the *atman*, is separate, inde-structible, in the same sense that Donne[29] has often pointed out and has really nothing to do with phenomenal reality. And that's kind of been blowing my mind. So as a result, I often spend several hours in the late afternoon, at which time my system is pretty much calmed down (I've given up eating lunch), so that around 3:30 in the afternoon, I start to get pretty high, and I usually spend a couple of hours sit-ting on the floor, very refreshing. When school ends shortly though, I would like to get out and do a little work. For the sake of the work, I've enjoyed collecting firewood from various building sites around here for the fireplace; and if I can get to know the Swedish people better, I mean the real Swedish people, the workers, I think it could be very valuable. Meanwhile this other professor is trying to line me up for this PhD scholarship for a new program in politi-cal science at the university. It's going to put me in a funny position if I get this scholarship, 'cause then I suppose I'll have to make a choice. But it's awfully hard to judge at this point whether what I'm going through now is temporary, or whether it just has something to do with being spring and toward the end of the academic year . . . it's hard to say . . .

Well, I suppose that's about all. Goodbye for now.

Bruce

Bruce, 2008–2009

By early 1969, I was broke and unemployed. Rosemary's income kept us afloat, but I wanted something useful to do and that did not include factory work. Rosemary knew about a graduate program out of the University of Stockholm, a master's program in public administration. The program was delivered in English and designed to attract foreign students. I applied for a student loan to finance living costs and add to our income for the little extras that made life bearable, such as bags of firewood.

---

29   John Donne, seventeenth-century metaphysical poet.

I had doubts about the value of an English-speaking master's degree in the Swedish labor market, but I did not want to go back to a factory job, like the disaster at the soap factory plant. So . . . I enrolled for the fall term of 1969, taking out a student loan.

Classes were held in Wenner-Gren Center, at the north end of Sveavagen, a major street stretching from the center of the city to the forested park of Kungsberg. It was where Rosemary worked, so sometimes we had lunch together. Wenner-Gren Center is a 243-foot tall glass and steel skyscraper that towers above its surroundings and appears taller than it is because it is not square, but rather a trapezoid shape that gives the roofline a soaring appearance. It was a center of international intellectual exchange and learning.

The effect was not lost on me. In elevated classrooms overlooking the city through large expanses of glass, I felt part of a world whose visions were lofty with learning and discourse. Reportedly, some of the best professors from the university's public administration faculty taught at the center, all with international reputations. The Swedes are proud of their public administration—they invented the ombudsman, the conscience of public accountability. I attended the lectures, read extensively, and wrote papers.

But my mood had changed. Although the professors were good to excellent, the students tended to the mediocre and I missed the intensity of intellectual engagement that I wanted. Most of the other students considered their year abroad as something of a lark and some were more interested in the bars and Swedish women than they were in the judicial administration of public matters, often arriving late for lectures, hungover.

There was a student council and I became active in it. With only a couple dozen students in the program from different countries, there for only a year, student participation was low. I easily became president. At a time when US university campuses were burning, according to the inflammatory news reports, I felt that the establishment-oriented atmosphere was out of touch with the times. I started to plan a takeover of the administration. I rounded up support among the handful of students who gave a damn about student council affairs and a showdown meeting was scheduled with faculty representatives.

The meeting went as planned; my cohorts and I prevailed in taking over the student council, according to Robert's Rules of Order. The faculty response was immediate and telling, "So—now what are you going to do—this is a university—we have freedoms—what exactly do you intend to do with this new majority in student council?"

I felt disillusioned in its true sense—stripped of illusion, seeing clearly the shape and shade of academic reality. I gazed beyond the horizon of woods to the north, through the plate glass windows of the top floor meeting room, and I could see that here was no different from elsewhere. All universities would be the same, all corporations the same, and governments to boot, especially governments.

I developed an intense anti-intellectual cast to my thinking. "What the fuck do you expect?" or "What the hell do you expect to accomplish with that (academic paper)?" were my watchword questions.

But worries about where my life was going and concerns about my future haunted my thoughts. I remembered an early spring walk along the north shore of Rasta, looking across the water to Sodermalm. It was a footpath through the woods along the water's edge. In spite of the sunny day, it was shaded with pine trees under the cliffs to the south. I was alone, and it was quiet. The sun was barely high enough to reach the water under the cliff's shadow. The ice appeared to be breaking up in the channel, but I did not notice any movement in the water or ice. Impatient for spring, in an impulsive gesture, I raised my hands to the sky and proclaimed, "Show me a sign!" To my great surprise, I heard the crashing of ice falling and a whooshing sound of water. Looking toward the water, I saw a channel marker bobbing back and forth like a metronome. It had been buried in the ice and only now had the melting allowed it to assume its upright position above its float and anchored counterweight. In a hushed awe, I watched it swing back and forth until it settled down. Only then did I notice the slight ripples around its base and knew for sure that water was on the move, east through the channel, through the Hammarby locks, out to the Shargarden and the Baltic Sea.

Alan, 2014

By the end of my junior year at Earlham in 1969, a dozen draft boards had been fire-bombed, the avenues of a hundred American cities set ablaze. In dormitories and classrooms around the country, armed students stood guard against college administrations whom they accused of collaborating with the military industrial complex. "America is a war zone," a friend told me. "Vietnam has been Anglicized."

A political science major, with whom I had unrequitedly slept, put it to me this way: "The police bash your friend's head in at the Democratic National Convention and he gets the best doctors, the best attorneys. He's dismissed as a hippie sowing his political oats. A black man gets his head bashed at the same demonstration and the world says, 'God help us! Another nigger with the absurd notion that he's free to express dissent.'"

We were lying together in a state of semi-nudity. She smelled like apples. "He can't afford a hospital," she said. "Can't afford a lawyer so they put him in jail as a terrorist. You may think two separate swords are chopping up America: the political one and the racial one. But there's only one blade—prejudice—and it doesn't lose its edge. It's been sharp for a long time. Imperialism or the Ku Klux Klan? It's the same sword underneath the hood and white robes." She stroked my cheek, said, "I gotta get dressed and go to class," and kissed my forehead.

Chapter Five
Knife at My Throat

LETTERS

15 July 1969
Taby,[30]

Dear Mark & Joey,[31]

You'll probably have to get Mommy to read this to you. I have been following with great interest the happenings in your house. I'm very sorry to hear of your daddy's problem (hemorrhoids); he might feel better if you made a joke; he can probably help you with that. Your mommy sounds terribly busy; good thing you cooperate by not spilling food!

Your Uncle Bruce and Aunt Rosemary have been enjoying the beautiful Swedish summer. Here the sun doesn't set until 9:30! How exciting that is when you have to go to bed right after sundown. Rosemary's sister, Karen, visited us . . . I got a kiss and a promise for my birthday, and Grandma and Grandpa Proctor sent money. Goody, goody. Rosemary and I will meet them in Norway, and then we'll travel. You know what travel is, Mark; remember the time in East Hampton? Your mommy can tell you if you don't remember. We will see fjords, mountains, lakes, Oslo, Stockholm, and Copenhagen. Aunt Rosemary has been working very hard. Uncle Bruce is working with older kids (the ones who go to school and

---

30 Suburb of Stockholm.
31 Mark and Joey Kozlevcar, young sons of Bruce's sister, Carol, and husband, Joe Kozlevcar.

ride bikes) whose real mommies and daddies go away. We've been having some fun times swimming, playing games, and eating. It's so much fun to eat with family. Happy Birthday to you, Mark. What did you get for loot? Remind Daddy to help you get something for Mommy next month. We will all drink a toast to you when the Proctors are together. (Drink a toast means to eat your toast and drink your milk.)

Your pals, Bruce and Rosemary

Bruce, 2008–2009

Having been in Stockholm for a year, I was missing some of my favorite food. Without my dictionary, I went off to a butcher shop to buy some pork spare ribs. My Swedish was rudimentary, and I wasn't sure how to proceed; I viewed the cuts on display. Some were close, but not the cut I needed for sweet and sour ribs. I pointed to the closest equivalent and said, in English, "Is it pork?" The butcher shook his head, hunched his shoulders and spread his hands open and up. I grabbed the butcher's hand, extended his index finger, and pulled his hand behind him near his bum. Then I pushed the back of his head forward. "Oink, oink," I said. The butcher began to laugh and called to his coworker in the back room. The two of them gazed at me and I put my hand on my ribcage, thumb and forefinger on the part of the ribs I wanted cut with an up and down motion of the two fingers along the ribs. Both were now laughing. Some conversation was attempted but the butchers didn't speak English and I was now too flustered to be coherent on any level. The cut the butchers offered was uncut ribs that looked like they might be pork. I nodded and this time they understood my pantomime of cutting them twice into shorter ribs. The butchers were really enjoying themselves by now and I thought that they were already rehearsing how they would tell their friends about this crazy immigrant who didn't speak Swedish and who tried to tell them what he wanted. Rosemary told me later that in Sweden pigs say, "Nuf–nuf," not "oink."

The island of Möja lies out in the skärgården, a large archipelago on the approaches to Stockholm from the Baltic Sea. The Swedes love their skärgården and in modern times it is a fantasy destination for summer vacations, whether for affluent sailors, or getaways to the *stuga*, the mythical cottage that almost all families have some access to. For the less fortunate, ferries leave from Stockholm harbor for day trips or overnight camping on some of the outlying islands.

Following the end of the spring session at university, besides visitors and traveling, I spent a good part of the summer of 1969 working as a counselor in a home for disturbed children who had become the responsibility of the state-run children's services department. A Swedish friend who was a social worker had provided a referral and the home needed some summer staff relief so that the regulars could take their summer vacations. The pay was minimal, but meals were provided and the prospect of being able to be outdoors in the short summer, rather than in a factory, warehouse, or classroom, seemed appealing. I was particularly excited about plans that the home had for a campout vacation on Möja, in the skärgården, over the midsummer holiday.

Midsummer is a big deal in Sweden, and as June 21 approaches, Swedes lay plans for debauchery, infidelity, or restful serenity. Although the sun sets, if it's a clear night, it never really gets dark and sometimes a dim red glow marks the northern horizon between sunset at 10:09 and sunrise at 3:30. It marks the beginning of the vacation season and many small shopkeepers close up and head for the *stuga*. Many factories shut down for three weeks in July. Brother Alan was backpacking before his stay with us and needed to repair his shoes; he couldn't get them repaired in Stockholm. Not a single shoe repair place was open. Tourists say that Stockholm is a lovely and quiet city. That's because nobody is there in July, except for the tourists and the skeleton crew that keeps the city operational. Any Swede who can heads for the country or, ideally, for the skärgården. Immigrants willingly adjust to this practice, if they can afford it.

I met other staff and kids at the passenger-ferry dock in Stockholm for the camping trip to the island of Möja. The boat was full as it headed east out of the main channel in blazing morning light—not a cloud in the sky, clear blue, reflected in the water, not even a hint of air pollution. I was jubilant—to be in a boat again, the kids the responsibility of the crew and others—free to gaze at the granite cliffs, spotted and streaked orange from lichen, the deep green pines along the crests and in the notches, the other boats, docks, buoys, and the receding skyline of Stockholm. Hardly a care in the world . . . I didn't know what lay ahead.

The ferry arrived at Möja just before noon, after hours of threading its way through narrow channels, between islands, occasionally pulling in to a small dock where groups of people would step off with their knapsacks and bags of groceries. The largest group got off at the main dock, along with the staff, kids, camping gear, and other light freight. The kids were issued prepared lunches and the other staff and I went to the local *konditori* for coffee and vienna bread, rich in butter between the flaky layers of dough, with a hint of marzipan. A pickup truck was arranged to carry the gear and groceries to the campsite. Most of the staff and kids walked the mile from the dock up a single-lane dirt road with grass between the ruts. It was a warm summer day, but the mosquitoes were not out. I sweated in the sun and coaxed some of the younger kids along.

The campsite was tiny—a spot of relatively flat ground among the crowned granite top of a small round hill—a *torp* in Swedish. To the northeast, over a crest, it sloped down to the water. In the lee of the *torp*, the slosh of waves on the rocky shore was all that could be heard. That evening's meal was basic camp—canned beans, hot dogs, and buns, prepared over an open fire. It had taken several hours to collect enough firewood for the meal and the evening's fire. The heath-like landscape was devoid of trees this close to the weather side of the island, and the rutted road appeared to follow the edge of what had once been a pasture. The late-evening light was still strong when a band began to set up their equipment in a small clearing at the base of the *torp* campsite next to the road. Soon, dancers began to arrive in pairs or small groups—a midsummer dance on the heath. As twilight approached, the wind dropped, and the mosquitoes came out. The other staff left me in charge of the kids and wandered off, not saying whereto, but I did not see them go down to dance or listen to the music. I thought that they must have friends somewhere close or were headed back to the dock and perhaps a screened porch to get away from the bugs.

Sitting around the campfire with mosquitoes swarming around our heads, I complained of the bugs, slapping myself in the face when I felt their sting and receiving a subtle rebuke from one of the older kids that, if you live here, you learn to take it. The younger kids did not need to appear brave and most of them retired to their sleeping bags with hoods drawn over their heads.

I thought I might go crazy and my arms would tire from slapping mosquitoes. The sounds of the party and dancing below us grew louder as the sun sank lower. It was clear that many below were drinking something much stronger than beer and the incessant om-pah-pah of the band sounded like what you would hear in a German beer hall, not on an idyllic island in the skärgården. With my face smeared in blood and smoke from the fire burning my eyes and nose, I understood why the staff had been so accommodating with me—leaving me with a bunch of sniveling, ill-tempered kids on a barren hill swarming with blood-hungry bugs. I longed for a drink and the revelry below only made my desire more pathetic. As the evening light grew gloomy, the band began to lose the beat and the accordion player was noticeably slurring the tempo and dragging the melody into a parody of music, more like he was tuning his instrument while the other members valiantly tried to uphold the beat. Suddenly the band just quit. The silence that followed was long enough for some of the dancers to shout their objections, but to no avail. The only sounds that now floated up to me were a couple of men in drunken fights, not pursued for long—the combatants had lost their will and coordination to the alcohol, and perhaps their dates as well, to more sober suitors. I could not imagine disappearing into the adjoining woods behind the bandstand for sex. To expose your skin under these circumstances seemed both foolish and dangerous to health. Perhaps the already thin crowd had snuck off to a screened porch or, if they were sane, to a mosquito-proof bed.

With the fire just a bed of coals, the kids tucked in, and nobody trying to sneak off to the party below, which was now dead, I huddled in my bedding and slept fitfully through the murky light of a midsummer night. I dreamed: a giant mosquito perched above me, its legs astride me, its siphoning snout probing for a hole through to my sweaty flesh for blood; a starless sky speckled with the embers of a disturbed fire, punctuating and offsetting a vastness of space, indifferent and ego-destroying, until there was nothingness, nowhere to appeal and none to listen, if I had felt the urge.

I was awake by four, the sun was up, a seaside coolness and dew suffused the campsite. Others stirred but did not rise. No other staff was in attendance. I itched and smelled. My hip was sore from sleeping on a rock. I knew my duty (from days in the Boy Scouts): gather firewood, make a fire and breakfast. I considered last night's ordeal and concluded that this was my life, better than being in Vietnam where my nightmares would have been my reality.

West of Stockholm lies Malaren, a large lake with numerous islands. It drops by mere meters through two channels around Gamla stan, the medieval center of trade and home to artisans. On the shores of Malaren, well outside Stockholm, the children's agency had a retreat, with several summer houses for the kids and staff. The resident psychologist had her own quarters and other staff lived with the kids, cooked, and kept house. The lazy days of summer in a bucolic setting were a relief for all from the city, but boredom soon set in, as the available day walks were repeated once too often.

It was there that I befriended a nine-year-old boy named Olaf. I was only recently aware that I had become Olaf's friend and I never knew why any of the kids had become wards of the state. Olaf seemed quite normal and I assumed that he had been orphaned. Olaf was sitting with me on the floor of the largest house's living room, taking a break from the breakfast cleanup. A 12-year-old girl, Ingrid, and one other male staff member, Gunnar, were lounging around and discussing plans for the day. I could tell from the demeanor of the other staff that something was up. An aggressive restlessness seemed to possess the kids.

Olaf said, "I want to go see Marguerite," referring to the resident psychologist.

"She doesn't want visitors," Gunnar said, "she's on vacation."

"I want to see her anyway," Olaf said.

Gunnar walked to the front door and gazed across the meadow to the psychologist's quarters. "She's not there anyway, her car is gone. She must have gone to town."

Ingrid was taking out the vacuum cleaner and she headed for the fireplace. Gunnar intervened to stop her and explained to me that Ingrid had once put the vacuum head into a live fire, setting the machine ablaze with its forced draft, spewing thick smoke into the air and almost setting the house on fire. In my concentration on understanding the dynamics of this situation, I did not notice that Olaf had snuck up behind me until I felt a small hand on my forehead, drawing back, exposing my throat to the feel of a sharp edge. My instincts from karate training told me to eliminate the threat of the knife by grabbing it with one hand and using the elbow of my other arm to swing around and dislodge the position of the assailant. I hesitated and looked up into the eyes of Gunnar sitting opposite me. I knew that Gunnar was a full-time, year-round employee who had more knowledge of how to deal with these kids than I did. Gunnar looked alarmed and said, "Olaf, you know that knives are not allowed, put it down."

Before Gunnar had finished this sentence, I felt all my senses heightened, suddenly aware of the early sunny day, the wind blowing in through the screen door, the sight of Olaf's small head behind mine reflected in the living room window, the location of Ingrid, also behind me, next to the fireplace, too far away for a joint attack. The entire scene froze, time stood still, and my mind seemed to rise above me, viewing this scene from above and through the ceiling. The small hand on my forehead hesitated and I felt my body begin to relax into the increasing alertness of a yogic trance. I now knew that the knife was too little, too dull, and Olaf was too small to do serious damage. At worst, my trachea would be severed along with the skin over it.

"Olaf, I thought you liked Bruce," Gunnar said.

"He is a coward," Olaf said, with feigned contempt.

"You do not want to hurt him," Gunnar said.

I sat motionless, but the pressure on my forehead weakened and my head slowly came down, my throat enclosing the blade with additional flesh and the muscles of my neck, now warming the small cold hand that held the knife.

"He is not worth hurting," Olaf said, withdrawing the knife and pushing my head aside. "Give me the knife," Gunnar said.

Olaf again hesitated and, still sitting, I swiveled around to look into the boy's eyes and, with a smooth and unrushed movement, raised his arm and took the knife away.

"It's not much of a knife," I said as I felt the edge of the pocket knife's three-inch blade, both dull and rusted.

"I found it in the dirt," Olaf said, as the tension and drama dissipated.

Gunnar looked skeptical and asked, "Shall we take a walk?"

Once outside, the kids went ahead; Gunnar and I followed well behind.

"I can't believe that you didn't defend yourself," whispered Gunnar.

I thought a moment and said, "I don't believe it either."

"He has cut other people."

"He didn't cut me."

"Are you a pacifist?"

"No."

"Then why did you let him do that?"

"He didn't hurt me."

My Swedish was not good enough to express the other things that I was thinking, not knowing if they were true. Others had likely been violent with Olaf. Had he become aggressive in defense? Did frustration trigger such episodes? Had he been accused of being a coward because he had given up fighting back against bigger, violent adults?

In August, we returned to the home in a suburb of Stockholm. The old home was a large two-story manor house with gaping windows in the Mansard style. The building had been extensively renovated and had a large, modern kitchen. It had once been the center of a sizeable estate and two rows of trees still stood nearby marking the old driveway into the house. Otherwise, the surrounding fields had been subdivided and were now filled with new detached single-family homes or side-by-sides. A lake and walking trails graced the surrounding public space. I was looking forward to the end of this summer job. The pay was lousy, and I had been reprimanded for taking food from the kitchen, even though I had thought that the job provided food. The school-year routine would begin soon, and the kids suffered from the end of summer "don't know what to do" blues.

By this time, I had learned more about Ingrid. I was astounded by the tales of periodic vandalism. Locks had been installed on the kitchen doors to prevent food raiding. Several times she had locked herself in the kitchen, put toothpicks in the locks so that she would not be interrupted, and proceeded to pour dozens of pounds of flour and eggs onto the floor, mixing them up with her feet and then scooping masses into the sink, plugging the plumbing, then turning on the water. Finally, staff managed to remove the pins on the inside door hinges. Ingrid then bolted through the outside door and ran around the house, picking up stones and throwing them through the windows.

Once, following this, I had overnight duty. Gunnar took care to get the kids in bed on time and, before leaving, advised me to lock the door to the main floor office that had a bed in the far corner for overnight staff. I retired and read in bed, leaving the door open so that I could hear if the kids were up and to no good. All was quiet and, tired from a long day, I decided that I would rather be able to hear what was going on in the house than not, so I turned off the light and quickly fell into a deep sleep. I was awakened in the middle of the night by a sound and, opening my eyes, I saw Ingrid and Olaf silhouetted in the doorway to the office.

"What are you doing up?" I asked, not wanting to rise from my warm bed. The kids only giggled as they fiddled with something between them. Then a box of wooden matches sailed through the air at me, all ablaze, tumbling through space, spewing dozens of sizzling points of flame. I was on my feet by the time the last matches hit the floor, just short of my bedding. In bare feet, I danced around the few matches still burning on the wooden floor and managed to get them out by slapping them with my book.

By this time the kids had fled in laughter and again all was silent. I choked on the smoke and then listened intently—nothing. I was amazed that the two had fled so silently. I ventured out into the adjacent living room, seeing and hearing nothing in the gloom. I avoided the light switches and glided through the rest of the main floor, then stood at the bottom of the stairs with my hand on the railing. I stilled my breathing, listened. There was a slight ruffle from above and then nothing. I stood frozen for a good five minutes . . . nothing.

I returned to the office, cleaned up the matches and sat on the bed. I waited and thought. I wondered whether to call for back-up, whether to close and lock the office door. I did neither. Instead, I sat on my bed in a lotus posture and decided to wait. I felt rested and, now calm and alert, I waited for sunrise.

When I told Gunnar about this incident the next morning, he told me that the two kids had done this same thing before and that was why he had advised me to close and lock the office door.

I did not return to work after this, and I did not call them either. They called me. "We need you here," said Marguerite.

"I'm not coming in," I said.

"It is your obligation to finish the terms of your contract—you owe us some hours yet."

"So, don't pay me," I said.

Chapter Six
Blue Collar Immigrant

Bruce, 2008–2009

Rosemary and I lived in Taby that summer—a modern walk-up apartment. A friend wanted an apartment-sitter while he went south on vacation and the rent was almost nothing. Best of all, he left us his car. "Can I take trips with it?" I asked.

"Take it wherever you want," he said.

I looked the car over. It was an old VW Beetle, even in 1969. "Is it OK on the highway?" I asked.

"Sure, it goes along just fine . . . I wouldn't take it outside of the country, though . . . the insurance may not apply. The right front end may need some work, but not now."

"Great . . . great," I said and fantasized about motoring through the countryside, camping wherever I wanted to.

And just then, Alan showed up with Gay, his girlfriend. She proudly showed us their crayon-stenciled images of tombstones they had made in English countryside graveyards. But first, Rosemary and I wanted a break. Let's go camping . . .

Alan, 2014

After my 1969 spring semester's "junior year abroad" in London, my college girlfriend, Gay, and I hitchhiked all over England and northern Europe. We took the ferry from Newcastle upon Tyne, England, to Bergen on the Norwegian coast and continued hitching to Oslo with a trucker who played Johnny Cash songs nonstop, and then on to Stockholm to visit Bruce. It didn't occur to me that our arrival came at an inappropriate time. Bruce and Rosemary were cordial enough not to mention that they had other plans . . . We stayed with them for nearly a week and then went north to Yokkmokk. Gay and I wanted to be able to tell our friends back in the states that we had traveled above the Arctic Circle. Bruce had warned us about the mosquitoes we'd find up there—and he was right. They were the size of locusts.

Bruce, 2008–2009

. . . It was August and I wasn't going back to work at the home. I began to lobby Rosemary for a trip. She was up for it and got permission to take her first vacation since she had started work at SIPRI. We bought a tent and a small cook stove and borrowed what was needed to cook. I washed the borrowed VW at the curb to our apartment building, checked the tires and fluid levels. I had owned a Beetle in the United States and was delighted to be able to drive again.

LETTERS

5 September 1969

Dear Eric,

Mostly we've been wondering about two things. Have you heard from the draft board?

1) Where are you? Somehow September is always fateful. We have moved again. New address: Storsvangen 129, Hagersten, Sweden. It's a cute farm house. We have the first floor and are sharing with Vesna, Rosemary's friend from Yugoslavia.

It's been a very exciting summer for us. Karen[32] took us a bit by surprise and left us feeling older than our years. She certainly is energetic. We drove down to Copenhagen

---

32   Eric and Rosemary's sister.

and had some fun there at the Tivoli. Then an old friend of Rosemary's visited: Amy and her new husband. Then, brother Alan and his girlfriend, Gay. They stayed six days! My parents topped it off. That we really enjoyed. We met them in Norway and spent a week and a half on the road with them. Norway is magnificent!

In capsule form that was it. The summer is almost over. In Sweden that means you fall asleep until next summer.

Your letters raised many questions. Perhaps most are no longer relevant. Personally, about family (especially fathers), sex, the bomb, etc. etc., I find that their relevance depends on posture, breathing, diet, and to a limited extent, environment. I don't subscribe to the division of body and mind made in the West; i.e., I think problems are manifestations of disequilibrium in the system, their resolution is an internal process, the manifestation of God (*Ātman* in Sanskrit) within us. How is knowledge known? By whom? If two people had to start all over, would it be the same? I don't suppose those questions deserve answers; perhaps meditation. You asked Rosemary, "At what principles have you arrived for ordering your life?" I don't think she has an answer; nor do I, really, except for the vagueness above. The assumption to the question is that life is addressed by principles. Is this true? Could such a belief be a mask to true perception of the nature of reality and thereby our place in it? I've always had a somewhat philosophic turn of mind. Sometimes it helps to answer letters, pragmatically speaking.

The colony stuff grew out of our recognition that many of our family and friends were seriously alienated from America. We thought if we went to Canada, we just might end up with a colony. You know, something along the line of "Home is where the hassles aren't."

Love, Bruce

24 September 1969

Dear Mark,

. . . I'm enjoying work now—less pressure to do boring things which make me nervous.

My stomach feels great, and I've stopped worrying about everything except Bruce, and am trying not to worry about him. He is supposed (according to plan) to take an exam in October on four books for beginning his master's degree work—quite difficult and full of details. But he isn't doing the reading, says it's not worth it, what good is a master's degree, etc. OK, so I've come around to, "he doesn't do anything really, visits friends, reads an assortment of things." I just wish he had something that interested him, something that he could get involved in. But he doesn't seem to have anything like that, and the thing is I'm finally realizing that it is much harder for him to be in that position than it is for me having him in that state of mind. So, I don't think he is very happy or anything.

We are talking quite seriously about coming to Canada eventually, but no settled timetable . . . Please tell us about your plans, trip, etc. Wish terribly much that we could see you, but at the same time I am so afraid I've changed so much—it is very hard for me now to make contact with friends from the states. Please write soon.

Love, Rosemary

26 September 1969

Dear Mom and Dad,

. . . I feel a little overwhelmed by this electric typewriter here at SIPRI on a Sunday afternoon, but I will try not to let it discourage the most molasses style that the free-flowing fingers fornicate. I can sincerely say that the impetus to self-sustained scholarly pursuit seems to have left me, if indeed, I ever possessed it. Perhaps for awhile. In the direction of political science, it certainly is not very fruitfully reaped (whatever that means). The upshot is that I just can't seem to take very seriously the whole idea, so I'm dropping it for now. Tomorrow I start some job, I really don't know what it will be, but it's just temporary until November 3 when I start a six-week course that will teach me to be a taxi driver. That should be fun and keep me out of trouble. Not that I've been in trouble, but I haven't exactly been out of trouble either. Wrong dichotomy, I guess. A friend tried to tell me it was a matter of pride. If you understand that, perhaps you can explain it to me. Rosemary and I are looking forward to a week or so vacation in Austria or Switzerland sometime this winter to go skiing and soak up a little sun . . .

I am waiting for Goswami's yoga book to arrive, so I don't do anything stupid to myself like I almost did a couple of weeks ago. So much for that. I see the doctor for the second time tomorrow about my head (skin infection). It looks all better to me now. I've been using two kinds of lotion, and a plastic bag over my head every night. I cut all the hair off, but I guess I already told you that . . .

Now we wait for the snow, so we can go skiing after work, on the weekends, etc. A season for every sport. We've been listening to the same tape over and over again due to our lack thereof. Perhaps we can afford tape now that I'm going back to work. We have been most encouraged for the sake of Alan and Eric about the cancellation of two months of draft calls this fall and the evident threats by Nixon that he will reform the system by executive order if he doesn't get his way with Congress. That may not be necessary since I hear Congress would prefer that anyway. Maybe they'll settle for the usual legislative permission. Now people are beginning to ask what kind of a military we want. I still don't think the general public appreciates the inordinate influence of the military in foreign policy. I didn't teach my high school government class the structure and character of the

Joint Chiefs of Staff for nothing. Oh well, a man for every season, a fragrance for every occasion. Before I drift off into a haiku, perhaps I should add that Eric is apparently wanted by the system sometime this fall. His reaction so far has been to seek a job as a nurse-trainee in a small hospital in New Mexico. Rosemary just handed me an article on the "poverty of American political science" . . . ! It is a beautiful sunshine day and the leaves will turn in one week and be gone in two.

Bruce and Rosemary

October 1969

> Like a long and lonely song
> That is practicing to die
> Dreams of childhood go floating by
> Like the sight of empty skies
> To a hungry wolf
> That has decided not to howl
> I think of Thee
> Thy Rod and Thy Staff
> They metaphor me.

. . . Yes, I can write political propaganda: soon, perhaps: I shall be baptized. Damn sin and protestant ethic! . . .

Bruce

6 October 1969

Alan . . .

. . . Just the mention of Cape Cod and East Hampton was enough to blow my mind. When I think of those places

I get so choked up that I am tempted to vow that I will return, but usually end up in a posture instead . . . Susan Sontag's long letter from Sweden in *Ramparts* speaks for many Americans who have been here without being here. If that doesn't outrage you: last week working in a light-bulb factory, warehouse division, watching the men and the work, doing the work and thinking with my hands and unfortunately with my back; trying to maintain equilibrium by often getting off my feet; doing shoulder-stands on top of packing crates, etc. One guy works with his dog. One guy looks like a distinguished school teacher, graying temples, magnificent frame, beefy face, in a working frock; seen after work carrying briefcase and wearing sports clothes. Who is he? Business executive? Not a year over 45 (later I find out he's 65, unloading crates off railroad cars, somebody had to do it, and I finished it) explaining in decent English that he remembered a little from his school days 40 years ago, and "I don't blame you" about the war; another short and stupid guy ("American? Can you drive a car there? Is it hard to get a job there?") who was usually stuck with the dirty jobs, had the most fantastic open little-boy face, like a dog with an angry master.

. . . Went camping three days ago out on the Baltic coast right after parents left, no energy to follow to Copenhagen; beautiful campfires late into the night, gazing at milky way. Moved again, oh well.

As ever, Bruce

Late October 1969

Dear Folks,

. . . I have temporarily abandoned studies here in Sweden. There were serious problems of motivation and relevance. A good part of it was that I never was seriously interested in political science. You may remember that I was doing graduate work in American studies before I was activated. So, I have gone back to work. I am currently working at a lumberyard stacking lumber that is dumped out of a saw. Several weeks ago, I was working at a light bulb factory in the warehouse section. Now I am trying to get into a government-sponsored retraining program to study to become a taxi driver, but I may have set my ambitions too high . . . Rosemary and I have been thinking more and more about Canada, specifically Vancouver. It seems to offer the scenic, recreational, climatic, and professional opportunities which would best suit our long-range plans . . .

Love, Bruce

23 November 1969
Soder

Dear Folks,

The greatest news from us is that we have found a new apartment, and for the first time, it's one we don't have to move out of at any definite time . . . It fits the description of the Gamla stan place; five floor walk-up, no central heating, but with an electric element and *kakelugn* wood stove (also *two* gas burners in the kitchen), no hot water but we plan to install a water heater, just a toilet and no tub, only the kitchen for a sink. The rent is $28/month, and it's all ours . . .

In the last 10 years, I have lived in around 30 different places. My employment record doesn't look much better. It's beginning to look like the personnel man's headache, the unstable personality . . . I have a hat with a wide brim I picked up in a secondhand clothing store that is about 20 years out of date. People on the street get a real kick out of it. Occasionally I get a warm smile from an old guy in his sixties who knows how silly it is not to wear a good hat (just like the one he's wearing) . . .

(Unsigned)

Alan, 2014

Although Bruce was 4,100 miles from his old Washington, DC, apartment, he was not disenfranchised from the American counter-culture. In an undated and unsigned letter, he reproduced by hand the Beat writer William S. Burroughs' poem, "Word Authority More Habit Forming than Heroin," as it was published in the Fall 1967 issue of *The San Francisco Earthquake*, a countercultural literary icon. In the poem's rib-kicking syntaxt, format, and police brutality, Bruce seems to be summing up the creeping inevitability of his isolation. One short paragraph ends the letter:

> Leafing through Rilke's *Letters to a Young Poet* and discov-ered, by his criteria, I don't have to write. Now standing in the post office realizing that in addition to not having to write, not having anything to say. Still planning on Montreal in mid- to late-August and then points west.

Bruce, 2008–2009

I learned over the summer of 1969 that I was not destined to be a social worker and did not want to work in the trenches of homes where I could be set ablaze or have my throat slit to qualify for a decent wage, eventually . . . maybe, if I could take an undergraduate degree in social work. What to do next? That was the question con-fronting me in the fall of 1969. By now I knew that my chances of getting any kind of "professional" work were almost nil. I discussed it with Rosemary, she asked Bert and Lillemore, and they suggested that taxi driving might suit me.

The income was above the average industrial norm and you would be outdoors, get around the city, working on your own. And

I knew how to drive, even enjoyed it—but was my Swedish good enough?

"You'll learn what you need to learn in the meantime," Bert told me. "Your Swedish is adequate, you can go to the taxi school; just like language training, it's tuition-free and you get a living allowance and train pass to the school out in the burgs—it's in the technical institute out there. But first you must go downtown for an interview with an employment counselor at the *Arbetsmarknadsstyrelsen* (labor exchange commission). Tell them that you want to be a taxi driver, that's your employment goal. You see, they are short of taxi drivers. But you don't have a job now, and they would much rather take you from a job with a surplus labor force to one with a shortage. So, you should say that you really want to work and that you'll take any job while you wait for a place in the taxi driver school."

By the time *Woodstock* the movie arrived in Stockholm in the fall of 1969, its reputation had preceded it. "What is this?" the Swedish popular press wondered, having only a year to try to figure it out. In the Underground network, it was a must-see.

"Meet me in the parking lot by the theater," said Gunnar.

"OK . . . see you there," I said.

So . . . Rosemary and I met Gunnar and several others under the trees at the edge of the lot. "You have to have some of this hashish," someone said. I accepted hesitantly.

As the curtains of night were falling . . . twilight time, we made our way across the parking lot, joined up with others, friendly salute, brothers known, through the theater's entrance and into our seats, two-thirds of the way back from the screen on the left, sitting side-by-side.

The tunes sent the hall a' rolling—blasting blues—rockabilly bounce and bop, feet a' pumpin' to the rhythm—the entire row of seats a' rockin' to the roll of music, summer 1968, WOODSTOCK!

Our six seats were the only ones rocking with the music. All the Swedes were respectfully watching this North American cultural expression, not rocking with it, not expressing anything with their bodies, withholding judgment . . . European intellectuals, Swedes included, debated whether the meaning was in the people or the music.

I was floored . . . two months after we had fled, this was filmed. *Carry on, Jesus, carry on*, I thought.

So, I went to the cab-driving interview in September. They spoke Swedish. I stumbled over many of the questions and even more so the answers. I did OK in confirming my employment and studies over the previous two years. I managed to convey my conviction that all I wanted to do in life was to drive a taxi and that I would do any job in the meantime, if I needed to wait for any preparation to becoming a Stockholm taxi driver. I guessed I must have made a credible case, because the counselor finally said, "So you want to be a taxi driver?"

"Yes," I said, and the counselor left the room, saying he'd be right back, and I waited maybe 10 minutes.

The counselor returned. "Well," he said, "the next class for taxi drivers starts in November." In the meantime, they needed a hand at a sawmill.

I went home on the subway from downtown to the suburb of Stureby, a 20-minute ride.

There was a 10-minute walk to the subway station near the house that Rosemary, Vesna, and I had recently rented. The next morning, I set off for the subway station and, after transferring just once, I arrived at the sawmill subway station. I walked another 10 minutes from there to the sawmill. It was in an industrial area in southwest Stockholm. On the last stretch, I noticed that it was on Lake Malaren, and looking down the *torp* to the lake, I could see the buildings by the water, idyllic in the afternoon sun. As I got nearer, approaching the squat building that had an "office" sign, I saw a large dirt yard filled with stacks of lumber, forklifts used to move the stacks around, a large, low building by the water, and what looked like a high square wooden grain silo adjoining it.

The office was dark and drafty. There was a table and chairs, a coffee urn, and some newspapers and magazines spread around—for coffee breaks, as I was to learn. The warmer "private office" of the manager adjoining the big room was where I was interviewed. The manager seemed only interested in confirming that I was who I was. "You're the one the labor exchange sent," he said.

"Yes."

"We work from seven to four, five days a week."

"Fine," I said and waited. As the manager looked me over, I wondered, *so . . . what next?*

"Do I have the job?"

"You start tomorrow morning," the manager said.

I was happy as I returned home to Stureby. I had a job and some prospects of things getting better. The walk home was in the late sunlight of a fall day. The maples were splendid yellow and other trees red along the suburban street to my single-family detached house. *Things could be a lot worse,* I thought.

The next morning, I arrived at the sawmill by seven o'clock, wearing my new work boots. It was mid-September and still warm enough. I had on a sweater and cotton smock and was shown to the inside of the big, low building that housed two saws. I was taken to the larger and learned that it could plane and cut four sides in a single pass through the saw. The saw was set up to plane and cut tongue and groove one-by-sixes—to be used in making forms for concrete. The Swedes poured a lot of concrete in constructing apartment buildings, bridges, and other structures. I was shown to the "ass end" of the saw where a long extension held the boards after passing the rough-sawed lumber through. The supervisor asked the other worker at the head of the saw to pass a board through. Through it came, wailing and spitting chips that were sucked down through ducts. Below the floorboards a powerful diesel engine turned a chip and dust extractor to take away the waste, and I was later to learn, pumped it through a pipe to the top of the tall building that looked like a grain silo.

"Here," the supervisor said, "you take the board and pile it on this dolly, and the next board next to it until the first layer of boards is down—then you keep stacking the boards up until the dolly is full. Then you start on a new dolly." Then the supervisor left, but he returned soon, just as the dolly was getting full and he showed me how the boards had to be laid down evenly, so the tongues and grooves would not be broken and the whole pile would be stable.

"What do I do with the dolly when it is full?" I asked.

"Someone will bring a new one."

I soon found I had to move the full dolly out of the way by hand and then roll in a new dolly so that the saw worked as continuously as possible. It was repetitive work and the saw was noisy, but I soon got into the rhythm of it, driven by the speed of the saw to keep the boards moving onto the dolly. Another worker from the yard would bring empty dollies and take away the full ones with a forklift.

The coffee and lunch breaks seemed solemn, but the warmth of the office building was a welcome relief from the cold draft. All the workers knew each other too well and had little in common, so there was not much conversation. Some were curious about me and asked questions at first but seemed amused by my less-than-fluent Swedish. They did not speak English or did not wish to if they did. I noticed that the oldest worker, who ran the other saw in the shed (he made moldings and other smaller stock), was hard of hearing.

I asked, "Why does he not wear ear protectors?"—knowing that the old man worked quite close to the saw and that it was loud even from my station 30 feet away. I gestured with my hands over ears because I didn't know the Swedish word.

"What's that?" one of the supervisors asked, not fully understanding me.

"Job safety," I struggled to communicate and repeatedly banged the heel of my hand into my ear until it hurt and said, "Ouch!" I looked around and saw that the entire lunch-room crowd was now intently following the conversation and my gesticulations.

"Oh, ear protectors," the supervisor said.

I repeated the words in Swedish.

"Yes," he said, "where is the union on this?"—surveying the faces around him. There was no answer, just silence except for the ruffle of clothing as the bodies around him avoided his eyes and shifted position. They had understood this question, all right, and none would show any knowledge of the answer.

I knew there must be a union because there were dues deducted from my paycheck. "Not for me," I said, "for him," pointing to the old man.

Two days later, the old man on the molding saw was wearing ear protectors. He noticed that I had noticed, caught me looking, and flashed a big smile. It was the only time I ever saw the old man smile.

After a week or so, the supervisor came by where I had just finished stacking a dolly of wood, the saw went dead, and the feed man had no more, when the super said, "There's another job you might do." I followed him to the high wooden building that looked like a grain silo. We went through the door and—amazed, I gazed up into a half-empty cavern of space, under the roof of this towering structure.

"Now," the super said, "follow me up these stairs," indicating a narrow, dust-covered wooden stairway fastened into the right-hand wall of the building, ascending upward, perhaps two-and-a-half stories to the corner of the building, where it turned 90 degrees to the left to climb along the far side, only halfway up, where it ended, seeming to bend under its own weight at the end.

In the cavernous space to our left stood an immense cone-shaped pile of sawdust and chips, like a sand dune, but of cellulose, the output of that diesel engine chugging beneath the saw. The open end of an eight-inch pipe gaped above the top of the cone, near the roof.

Voila, I thought, *here is the saw's waste; here is where the exhaust of chips and dust goes; here is where it is stored—so . . . what next?*

The super explained, "Tomorrow, a big truck will come and suck all of this away."

"Where will they take it?"

"I don't know—to a factory that makes pressboard panels—mix it with glue and it's like a sheet of plywood, but of mixed fiber—strand board," he said.

"OK, what's next?"

"I want you to follow me up these stairs—now be careful."

I did so, noting the increasing level of sawdust on each stair as we ascended.

When we reached the corner of the building where the stairs turned left up the back wall, the super stopped and reached for a rake—not your ordinary rake—this one had a handle 25 feet long with a broad paddle on the end, buried in the chips below.

"When the truck comes tomorrow, I want you to be here, pushing the sawdust down toward the bottom. He will suck it up into his semi to take it to the factory. We are on contract to deliver. Can you do it?"

Can I do it?—I wondered. The question suggested that maybe I didn't have to—that it wasn't part of my job—that it was my option—maybe nobody else wanted to do it because there was an element of risk from falling and breathing the dust. "Yes, I can do it," I said.

"Good; don't fall into the chips; you will sink, like in quicksand."

I didn't understand the Swedish word for quicksand, but I understood the body language of the drowning super, hands waving overhead, gasping for air.

"And wear this." He reached for a dust mask hanging from a nearby nail. "They come tomorrow."

I rationalized, *the first time at anything is always a learning experience*, and so it was with the dust-sucker truck. When it pulled into the yard, I was alerted to take my station on the trapeze walkway with the rake tool. I stood at my post and the great door was opened, halfway up, like a Dutch door, open to the sky. The semi operator knew his stuff—a 10-inch pipe was snaked out and inserted into the pile. The main semi engine was engaged into the sucking mechanism and the pile began to cave in at the bottom, as if some worm was eating a sand dune from the bottom, causing the rest to cave in around it.

Aha, I thought, *my job is to feed the vacuum auger, keep it fed, and keep the chips a' moving.*

So, it became my weekly job—the sucker arrived—the sucking finished—I kept it movin' downhill—when done, stow the rake, dust off, hang up the mask, and back to the ass end of the saw.

Below the big saw that I worked on, and to one side there were some narrow, steep stairs that led down to where the sawyer had his work space. I was not allowed down there, but I could see hung on the walls were tools, saw blades, and planes. The sawyer was proud of his saw and explained that it could be configured to cut and plane four sides of wood up to eight inches square in one pass. In a hushed voice, he said, "There is someone who lives down there," pointing down to the stairs, "we call him the Gremlin."

Suspecting a joke, I said, "Did you say he lives down there?" The sawyer put his fingers to his lips and nodded.

"Why?" I asked.

"He has some problems," was the answer as the sawyer gestured and tipped a bottle back to take a long swallow.

The Gremlin who lived below the floor boards of the main saw, down where the sawmill engineer/mechanic worked, down where the diesel engine sucked the sawdust off to the silo, for delivery to the strand board factory, emerged. The occasion was the delivery of a boatload of raw-sawn lumber one-by-sixes, reportedly from Finland but, considering the small craft, the lateness of the season—and the storms that beset the Baltic in October—I thought that it might be from cutting areas around Lake Malaren. Disinformation was not a new game, even in the Swedish forestry industry.

The rest of the workers also emerged, but stood aside, as the Gremlin stood on the quay waiting for the boat to dock. The boat's deckhands had already slung a load of boards from the boom of a derrick mounted on the deck. The Gremlin waited for the first load as it swung in the wind, perhaps a forklift full coming over the railing, down toward the quay. The Gremlin tackled it, leaning his whole body against the momentum of the swing, his feet slipping on the frosty quay, the last of the day's sunlight disappearing from the glow on the horizon.

The four other workers waited, lined up in a row: the supervisor, two sawyers, and the main saw feeder. I waited, too. Load after load swung over the side, the small boat rocking after releasing the weight of each load, the hull's water marks rising above the murky lake. Still the Gremlin had at it, load after load. Nobody stepped forward to help. As the Gremlin began to stagger from exhaustion and who knows what else, I made a move to help and was stopped by a hand to the shoulder. "Do not go there," was the silent message.

My heart was large for this alcoholic, living under the boards, seldom seen, the deliverer of wood when the boat arrived, grist for the sawmill. When it was all over, the wood off-loaded, the boat's decks cleared, the farewells shouted between captain and quay, the message dockside was, "let the load lay . . . we will deal with it tomorrow morning."

That was the only time I ever saw the Gremlin.

And so, the rest of the crew dealt with it the next morning, but I did not help. I took my place at the ass end of the saw and stacked the tongue and groove one-by-sixes, with the doors to the quay closed. On the quay, they must have stacked it on dollies and stored it in the yard. Meanwhile, the lumber continued to show up at the mouth of the saw, the diesel chugged, the Gremlin was back in his hole, and the cycle was completed.

I worked for six weeks at the sawmill. Peter and Ingrid had convinced me to become a vegetarian and right before this job I had weighed 168 pounds. After six weeks, I weighed 148 pounds and was burning more energy in the progressively colder, unheated saw house. Returning home to Stureby one evening, Vesna seduced me with a goulash, not Hungarian but Yugoslavian—the secret is in the paprika—and it smelled wonderful and tasted even better. I awoke the next morning feeling rested and, for the first time I could remember, invigorated. The following day, I received a letter from the labor exchange. I had been enrolled in the taxi school in Sollentuna, a satellite town north of Stockholm.

I went to the appointed meeting downtown and the details were explained. I signed some forms and was told that checks would arrive, after I began school, for living allowances and to cover the commuter train to Sollentuna.

Chapter Seven
Taxi Driver

Bruce, 2008–2009

As I was riding the train north from Central Station I thought, *only in Sweden would they have a government-run taxi school and pay you to go.* I caught the connecting bus to the vocational school on the edge of Sollentuna.

I was impressed with the facilities: a large, well-lit triple garage with a high ceiling and chairs and a screen for projecting slides at the front. Best of all, there were three new four-door Volvo sedans painted black with taxi dome lights on the roof. There were two full-time instructors for the 12 students.

I soon learned that one was the good cop type and the other the bad. The other students, like me, were retreads: a welder who had injured his back, a housewife who needed money for her teenage sons. Some would make it to graduation and some would not. The ones who didn't make it were mostly the ones with emotional problems—cried in class, for example, when bad cop delivered a stern lecture about how to deal with drunks that puke in your cab. The housewife's husband was probably one of them and abusive to boot. She didn't make it to graduation.

The school cafeteria served coffee and a selection of sweet cakes for the morning and afternoon breaks, as well as lunch. Most of the other students in the school were high school age and, like all kids this age, there seemed to be a pecking order. The industrial mechanics and chemists seemed to be tops among the boys and the secretaries and stenographers tops among the girls. I couldn't say how I knew about this pecking order. Perhaps it was the way the taxi students always went to the cafeteria together and left together. They always sat together at the farthest end of the hall. No other students or staff ever approached our group. From our vantage point in the corner of the cafeteria, I watched.

At first, I struggled with the Swedish. In the beginning, there were a lot of lectures, the "ground school" equivalent of pilot training. It started to come together for me about a month into the course. This was technical stuff. Almost any concept could be explained with a graphic. The vocabulary was new but easily mastered—the names of road signs that meant *merge, caution, deer crossing,* and *do not enter.*

The fun part was the driving—just to be out and about seemed like a treat, and I mostly rode with the good cop. On one occasion, however, I was to drive the bad cop to a destination in Stockholm— just the two of us. This was unusual; we normally rode four to a car and rotated the driving. Near the end of the trip, the bad cop became friendly and talkative. On one stretch of good road with no traffic, the bad cop said, "You should speed up a bit, there's nobody around and the roads are clear and safe."

I glanced down at the speedometer and saw that we were going the limit. "I think I'll stick to the speed limit."

"No, go ahead, speed up a bit, I'm late for my appointment," said the bad cop.

"It's OK, I'll keep to the limit."

The good cop liked me. I was sure of it. In a moment when we were alone the next day, he whispered that I had passed the bad cop's test. Somehow, I knew that the bad cop was disappointed . . .

Bert wanted to see *The Good, the Bad and the Ugly.* He liked tough westerns. This one was highly rated. He wanted to treat me and Rosemary, so we went to a theater on the north side of Soder. I was particularly interested because I had known Eli Wallach (the ugly in the movie) from East Hampton.[33]

"Great movie," said Bert afterward, "what does it say about life?"

"Whaddaya mean?"

---

33 Eli, his wife, Anne, and their three children lived next door to our summer cottage on Three Mile Harbor. During World War II, Eli was a noncombatant working at hospitals in Europe. In 1970, he wrote a letter to the Norman, Oklahoma, draft board supporting my decision to register as a conscientious objector.

Bert explained, "Well . . . we have universal conscription . . . to the military . . . to defend Sweden against aggression . . . you have to do what you have to do . . ."

"Yes," I said, "that is true."

"And I really like happy jazz, not the sad stuff."

"You mean the blues."

"Whatever they call it . . . I like the happy jazz."

So, Bert saw America and its values through their film and music . . . westerns and jazz. Not a bad selection. I did not tell Bert that Eli supported American resisters to the Vietnam War. Bert identified with his Viking heritage. He was in the reserves and spent some weeks every summer on active duty at an undisclosed location. He mentioned the S-tank, an unconventional design that had no turret, but with adjustable suspension for aiming the main gun. I had also seen hardened bunkers for airplanes off a main road in southern Sweden. In the middle of a forested region, the road was suddenly wider, with the right-of-way cleared several hundred yards on either side. Taxiways, like entry and exit ramps, ran off the road to these bunkers.

I saw other signs of a fortress mentality in military preparations. Many rural roads that cut through rock would be barricaded, with a large steel gate swung open, ready to be closed with the approach of enemy forces.

Some of the resisters became Swedish citizens and were thus subject to conscription. One story that made the rounds in the underground network was about an American who was called in for a conscription interview; it went something like this:

"You are subject to be conscripted into the Swedish armed forces. There are several reasons that you might give for exemption. They include health, conscientious objection, and sexual orientation. Which would you like to choose?"

LETTERS

(December 1969—finished and mailed in January 1970)

Dear Alan,

Just a note. I passed the taxi driver's test . . . Will take a ski vacation in Austria before starting work. Thinking of going to Vancouver, BC, end of this summer or next summer. Sense of future time related to crisis of last letter and running out of dope. No dope is a trip; spread the word: four months on alcohol and tobacco and you're middle America. M.G. reports that middle America is more uptight about "free people" than it ever was about blacks. True? I understand Sweden is making a little news over there. H is back from 'Nam and J reports he's "changed." D is on a kibbutz after "a certain magic" in Marrakesh. At 26, I feel too old to care and too young to die; meanwhile I'm in the best shape since age 12, creepy skin disease notwithstanding. The Swedish consensus on communes is: Whose kid do I have to take care of this time? Do you ever wonder if you mean what you write, or are you:

1. testing a mood
2. waiting on
3. suffering
4. etc.

I think I was suffering the mood, so now, more than a week later and after a move and new year's (today is New Year's Day), it's changed. Recently I have been wondering about the cohesive forces of large industrial civilizations and have come to the surprising conclusion that all the boring answers are the right ones (accurate), i.e., we really do establish our collective identity through the organs which address themselves to that purpose. The matter of relationship, in this perspective, is irrelevant (credible!). To change the subject: I think camping is nice. Its opportunity for social learning is immense because nobody owns the woods, and all the everyday living routines must be created; having no traditions, except what one carries on one's back and in one's head—which is considerable—is better than most communes where there are either signs everywhere or no signs, and it takes considerable embarrassment and silent smiles to learn what is happening . . .

The more I watch people, the more I see them as children. The party last night: He: "Aw c'mon, gimme a kiss." She: "Oh you silly little boy," slappy facey. Re: experience. Assumption: You are me. Analysis: Schizophrenic. Meaning: Humanitarian. Significance: Commonly experienced phenomenon is equally perceived. Conclusion: You exist. Underlying significance: I have a hangover and haven't done my yoga since December 12, and in the interim I learned that pleasure is what society teaches us to feel when we are dying, that is, using up our body in pleasure . . .

I got sick at 2000 hours, December 19, 1969, and am just recovering. Luckily it comes once a year. I was forced to admit in the middle of it that I felt the spirit and was having fun. I was put through the ritual of de-relativizing time and judging the year, not to mention the decade. I hope that the foolishness is over now . . . Rosemary and I have enjoyed each other's company on vacation and will shortly bury ourselves in work and wait for Easter, my favorite holiday . . .

(unsigned)

December 1969

Dear Folks,

I'm answering your letter, Mom, of December 6 . . . We're not affiliated with any church; just the free-flowing existentialist ache of barren truth. Yes, (we need) canned goods, meats, and packaged goods. What do we miss most? Rosemary misses the people. I miss birds, singing, sun shining, surf, black people, open spaces, the justified resignation of living that comes from such a crazy social order. We are hoping that Alan gets laid and are in favor of his coming back to Britain; keep him mixed up for awhile, or was he ever? Enclosed are some snapshots. You can have the one of me taking a picture of me in front of your bedroom mirror to stick in that selfsame mirror, in the future to be called the magic mystery mirror . . .

The celebration of "Lucia" (song of St. Lucia), or the time of lights, has just passed under the old calendar winter solstice. The coming of light is symbolized by a maid (beautiful blonde chick), wearing a crown of holly and burning candles, who comes around and wakes you up; solemn, semi-religious, impressive. I missed it while sleeping on the desk on the 16th floor of Wenner-Gren Center. So much for native customs.

On books: if we need some, we'll tell you which ones. Have a merry Christmas. I'll open packages. Can't we look before breakfast!? Wash the dishes? Go away H, what did Dan give me; don't save the wrapping paper, man, it only covers it up.

Bruce

Alan, 2014

In the fall of 1969, the beginning of my senior year, longtime political loser Richard Nixon won the presidential election by appealing to "the silent majority." I thought of my parents: older, timid, ideologically progressive but practically conservative and looking for "law and order" amid the concussions of violence they saw nearly every day on their TV. My father was a captain in the naval reserves. He had never expressed an opinion to me about Vietnam. I had never asked—which was too bad.

In December of 1969, six months before I graduated from Earlham College, the Selective Service instituted a national lottery system that drafted males between the vigorous ages of 19 and 25. I was almost 22 years old. The draft was the administration's answer to a war from which 200,000 men had fled, either overtly or covertly. Demand for fresh meat couldn't keep pace with the available volunteers. The lottery assigned random numbers to birthdates, and that first year they churned through 195 unlucky birthdays. Mine—March 8th—put me at number 213 in the lottery. I was safe—at least for the time being.

I graduated with a BA in English in June of 1970. The class valedictorian, a brilliant young woman named Janet whose poetry had already been published, rose to give her address to the assembly of parents and students restless on the folding chairs set up in perfect rows on the grass. The audience fanned themselves with the programs. Janet came to the podium, leaned over the microphone, and waited for quiet.

Paraphrasing the concluding words of an anti-war poem by Bill Knott in his book *Auto-Necrophilia*, she said, "I don't understand anything. If you do, tell it to me real slow, in one-syllable corpses." Then she sat down. Clearly stunned, Landrum Bolling, the college president, in full black and royal-blue robes, approached the microphone and asked for a moment of silence.

This was my world in 1970. I was fresh out of college, eager to be on my own and wondering if my education would land me a job. My brother's world, in his second year of exile and struggling with life in Sweden, glimmered through a darker lens.

LETTERS

Early January 1970

Dear Raj,[34]

Thank you for your Christmas greetings. We were glad to hear that Mark is taking good care of you. The tapes you

---

34 Bruce and Rosemary's cat in Washington, DC, spayed a year previously.

bought for us certainly will fit the machine. We have moved yet again . . .

I suppose you are feeling your normal self now but may have noticed Mark a bit depressed. This is called the "after-Christmas, end of the year, where did-it-all-go and what-was-it-for syndrome." It is common among humans in January and even into February. It is partly their own fault; with all that good stuff to eat and drink, they reach the limits of body gratifications, get bored, and don't meditate. But maybe they'll learn from you someday. How did it come about that you were displaced as an object of worship in Egypt?

I passed the taxi test but am still trying to get a job; incredible doors to go through; not enough sunshine. We miss you and Mark, Washington, DC, 17th St., Highs,[35] Trio (french-fried onion rings and beer), central heating, English, being able to interact.

Our deepest love to you and your master; may you contemplate the reality in peace and recognize the dark shapes as mind.

Bruce & Rosemary

January 1970

Dear Folks,[36]

We have finally settled into our little room and kitchen with kerosene heat, and cold water but no bath. That's fun because then you can go and visit your friends and have baths there and when the door is locked look through their medicine cabinets and see what their heads are into. But sometimes we miss having our own shower. One friend named Peter has a big bath in his attic. That one's the most fun

---

35 A popular DC ice cream shop in Bruce's old neighborhood.
36 To Bruce's sister, Carol Kozlevcar, and her family.

'cause it's big and you can almost float, but I know some of you folk can do that anyway. It really doesn't pay to grow any bigger than your bathtub.

Aunt Rosemary is working too hard but will get a vacation soon. Uncle Bruce has started driving his taxicab. You never would believe how many people want to go where they're not. I think that everybody should just stay at home and send me the money through the mail. My boss says that's unrealistic. Big people like that word; watch out for it—and for authority. Those two are their favorites.

The electronic fairy tells me you have snow. Well, so do we, and skis! What we really need is sunshine. Could you send us some? Tell your parents we liked your presents. Aunt Rosemary's hasn't come yet, but the tape is always welcome. Rosemary's birthday is January 12 . . .

. . . This is a week later, and it seems your package is waiting in a post office to be picked up. Our Italian friends are being transferred to Paris, so we are happy to have someone to visit there. We're taking a weeklong ski trip to Austria March 1—a little place west of Salzburg in the Alps. I'm excited. Never been south of Copenhagen.

Love, Bruce and Rosemary

28 January 1970

Dear Folks,

. . . We have been worried about you, Ella Mae; perhaps it is time to slow down, and despite the old man across the street, that doesn't mean you'll stop. In the first place, activity is the antithesis of concentration, and it is concentration through which we achieve unity, either with our point or environment, the distinction disappearing in the higher stages of concentration. At such a point of stillness, the body verbalizes itself. As everybody knows, there comes a time when it arbitrarily decides to change forms: not matter. As for stopping smoking: I found that the attitude is more important than the habit, and precedes it, whether smoking or not. Personally, I found that the "high" I got from proper ventilation was more satisfactory than the light proto-narcotic effect of nicotine. You may wish to try this yourself: sitting back in a straight chair, comfortable but not leaning back, hands on thighs, relax the abdomen and breathe through the nostrils; in and the abdomen expands, out and it contracts: this is diaphragmatic breathing, do not use the musculature of the rib cage, panting is not correct. It usually helps concentration to have the eyes closed, but this is not necessary. Initially, you will find that it takes concentration to do this correctly, later the desire for the state of mind will be sufficient. A natural pattern will establish itself in the breathing, it should never be forced.

Thanks for the info on BC. I never realized it was that spectacular. And wild! I got a reply from the visa office here which said I had to get "the necessary evaluation" of my credentials to teach in BC, so I got a note off to Victoria within a day. Paperwork! Monday morning, I start driving taxi. That all started in October. Again paperwork. What I needed to learn to do the job could easily be mastered in three weeks. Maybe the real object is to test you with trial by time! You know: put up with the hypocrisy and bullshit for four years and we'll give you a piece of paper. I'm not really down on my education, but in retrospect I think I learned more in both junior and senior high school than I did in the university. I learned the most outside of class in my university days and in reality, thereafter. The obvious truth that all jobs must be learned after being hired seems to be a truth that is lost on everyone except those who are free to hire anyone. I could go on in this vein, but the system, I am learning, has its redeeming characteristics. The primary one is that it is a game. Somehow, reality remains the least relevant factor in social intercourse. And thanks for the subscription to *Saturday Review*, they do occasionally have good articles, but I feel that they are long on sentiment and short on facts, but always right. Just like a liberal . . .

Love, Bruce & Rosemary

A drawing of Bruce meditating.
Art by Ingrid Sedgwick, a Swedish friend.

Bruce, 2008–2009

Well, suicide might be painless, but the word was out on the underground circuit—the movie *M*A*S*H* was a must-see. So, a bunch of the guys went to see it. We were a little late in arriving, but there were six seats in the front row. Settling in, the movie just starting, the screen loomed large overhead, so we had to tilt our heads back to watch. Thankfully, it had an English soundtrack, with Swedish subtitles. The humor was black with lots of zingy one-liners.

It was eerie, because as the six of us became lost in the script and the quick jokes, we noticed that when we laughed, there would be a pause as the rest of the audience read the subtitle and then they would laugh. It was almost as if we Americans down front were telling the jokes and the audience responding, right through the movie. We let the Swedes know which were the funniest lines, getting the joke slightly before the rest of the audience, as if giving them permission to loosen up and enjoy it. I felt like a member of an evangelical chorus, with the congregation joining in with hoorahs echoing our laughter down front.

Of course, *M*A*S*H* was full of meaning and it wasn't just about the Korean War. We felt vindicated and justified. *I told you this war is the shits*, we thought. The only real meaning is in people's perseverance in the face of adversity, insanity, and brutality.

After graduation, I bought the required parts to my taxi uniform: a blue military-style hat with black brim, a shirt with blue tie, blue jacket and pants, and black belt and shoes. I had an appointment downtown at Taxi Central (an organization of independent owners that coordinated the reservation and taxi-radio systems) for training and certification for a taxi-radio permit. I wore my new uniform. The training was minimal, with some simulation and I passed the tests.

One of the chief taxi inspectors offered to show me around. I had heard of these inspectors, they could suspend or revoke your taxi permit. You did not say "no" to them. The inspector walked me around the premises. Over there, in the big area behind the glass, mostly women with headsets on, taking calls from people wanting a taxi. They would then find the closest taxi station (a phone on a post near the curb), call them, and the first taxi in the lineup would take the call. If there were no taxis at the station, they would use the radio. There was only one radio channel, so it could get busy during rush hour. You could always be waved down, as was often the case at night or on weekends downtown, or near the bars. "Over there," the inspector gestured, "is the radio room."

As we walked down a hallway, an excited older man in taxi uniform approached the inspector and began to plead. I could not understand all of it but gathered that the older man was desperately looking for a driver—he had recently bought a new taxi. Christmas was approaching, and he was exhausted from working 12 hours a day in order to make ends meet.

"May I introduce Bruce Proctor," said the inspector, "Bruce, this is Sture Carlson."

"Glad to meet you, Mr. Carlson."

The inspector said, "Bruce is a recent graduate of the taxi school and is looking for work."

Sture Carlson's face lit up with a huge smile and he held his hands up in front of him, elbows at the hips, in supplication, as if he were about to receive a divine child from the Pope.

So, I started driving for Sture Carlson, six days a week, the day-shift one week and the night-shift the next week. Once a month, there was a long day-shift that started at three in the morning. The streets needed to be covered 24 hours a day, but the traffic was slow in the early morning hours. Returning to the garage after the day-shift, Sture would meet me, ask how I was doing, all the time smiling, a perfect gentleman with his ruddy complexion and gray crew-cut, and he was a foot shorter than me. Once a week we would settle on my pay. It consisted of a percentage of the total money accumulated on the meter, plus a flat amount for each fare. Before and after each shift, I would make note of them. The tips were for me to keep, but 10 percent in income tax was due on them. Tips averaged 13 percent.

I was conscientious and hard-working—rarely called in sick or missed a day's work. I always had money in my pocket from tips and with my new wealth, I started smoking again. I had quit one-and-a-half years previously when I arrived because a pack of cigarettes cost $1, which I did not have to spare on a daily basis. (I had been paying $2 a carton at the Base Exchange.) With the sweet sound of change clinking in my pocket on the way home, I would often buy some smoked herring from street vendors or get a little something special for Rosemary. Life was good. I was getting to know the city and its surrounding suburbs, many of which I had never seen.

Sture was helpful when needed. I sought his advice on an argument I had with a fare. "Do not make the customer unhappy," Sture explained, "if there is an argument, turn off the meter and reach some agreement on the fare."

"But if I turn off the meter," I said, "the dome light on the roof will come on and the hand on the meter will be up, showing the taxi is free."

"I will show you something," Sture said, "use this only if you have to. Here, under the dash, is a little switch which shuts off the dome light even when the meter is off."

"Gee, I didn't know you could do that."

"Yes," said Sture, "I use it when I take the wife to the hair salon during the slow hours before lunch."

"Thank you."

Several days later, late at night and toward the end of my shift, I picked up a fare at a downtown bar. It was an American tourist and a Swedish woman.

"Where would you like to go?" I asked in Swedish.

The woman answered, "To Sollentuna."

I didn't need to hear more. I knew the way to the town north of the city where my taxi school was located. It would be a good fare, long distance in light traffic at high speed, the meter just a-whirring away. The two in the back seat were intoxicated but not to the point of puking, a taxi driver's worst nightmare next to a collision. I was confident they wouldn't puke since they had enough energy to be pawing each other once they hit the darkness of the rural road.

I gave all my attention to the driving and tried to ignore the moans and slurpy sounds of French kissing, wondering if they would try to get if off in my back seat. If that happened, at least the volume would be less than puking. Slowing down as we approached Sollentuna, I glanced in the rear-view mirror and held up the palm of my right hand, as if to say "Where now?"

The woman said, "straight ahead, on the right," freed herself from an embrace, leaned forward and said, "the tall apartment building up there," pointing over the seat so that I could see.

"Thank you for a wonderful evening," she said in English to her American companion as she opened her door.

"What . . . this is it?" he said, as he started to get out of the cab.

"You can't come up," she said, putting a hand on his shoulder to keep him in the taxi.

"But . . . I thought . . ."

"My boyfriend would not be happy," she said.

With that the man looked deflated, said "Fine," and slammed the rear door.

"Where would you like to go?" I asked in English, pulling away from the apartment's front door.

"You speak English?" the man asked.

"Yes."

"Shit—do you know where I can find a woman?"

"Here . . . past midnight . . . no," I said.

"Then back to the city, I guess. Shit . . . are all Swedish women like this?"

"Her call."

The man paused, bent forward and looked at the taxi meter. "Is there another way back, twice the meter is a lot of money."

"We can try the railroad station," I said, the meter still running.

At the railroad station I got out and found that the next train was not until early morning and told the man. "So, what do you want to do?"

"Let's go back to the city," he said, "but do I have to pay twice what's on the meter?"

"We can make an arrangement," I said, knowing that if the man had gone upstairs to the woman's apartment, I would be going back empty anyway. Besides, I was not allowed to pick up fares in Sollentuna, even if there were any on a late, dark night. So, an arrangement was made for a modest additional amount to what was on the meter. I accepted payment and reached under the dash for that little switch that turned off the dome light when I shut off the meter.

I knew I could keep the additional money and not have to report it, even for taxes. I was a happy camper, even though the American was grumpy for awhile. He soon seemed to get over it and turned his attention to me, saying, "An American, eh?"

"Yes."

"Where are you from?"

"Washington, DC . . ."

"What are you doing here?"

"Driving taxi."

"Yeah, but, how did you end up here? I mean . . . do you have family here, or . . . something else that brought you here?"

I hesitated. I had scoped this guy as a corporate or private business type. Often, these Americans were Vietnam War supporters. "Some of this and some of that," I answered, and that's about all the American got out of me, on a personal level.

I once had a fare to the airport with a suit-and-tie Spanish man who spoke fluent English. The conversation came around to Generalissimo Franco, then Spain's head of state. I said, "Isn't he allowing US bombers landing rights on their way to Vietnam?"

"Yes, unfortunately," answered the Spanish gentleman.

I waited, and then I said, "I mean . . . Franco is getting old. Times are changing . . . a change is inevitable. The voice of the Spanish people will eventually be heard."

"You are fortunate that you can speak your mind," the gentleman said, "In Spain, that is still dangerous."

Taxi school had taught me taxi etiquette. First, you are in uniform. You are there to serve the customers. You open the door for them. You help them enter your cab, if they need assistance. You are polite, always. I found that, in following this creed, my working personality was changing. I had never had to be so subservient before, not even while serving tables at a restaurant during my university days.

Service . . . that was the key. Swedish has a formal and an informal way of addressing people. Most Swedes used the informal "you" in conversation. However, if I picked up a fare in Östermalm, an old, rich neighborhood in Stockholm, I soon discovered that the customer in the back seat could easily take offense at my use of the informal pronoun. "Snotty old people," my friends would say when I told them stories about the lecture that I had received on proper Swedish grammar. "Where did you say you picked them up?"

"In Östermalm."

"Of course," was the reply.

After that, I noticed that the denizens of Östermalm would be quick to establish that, as an American, I didn't work for ESSO, IBM, or have some other reputable job with a multinational, so I must be "one of those," unspecified.

The tabloid newspaper in Stockholm was *Aftonbladet*. The editors liked bad stories about American deserters. The headlines almost screamed, "American Deserters Spreading Drugs Among Us," or "Deserter Beats and Kills Girlfriend."

I remember that Parker S., my high-school buddy who went AWOL to Stockholm in February 1968, did a content analysis master's degree thesis with the University of Stockholm on the press coverage of American deserters. I never read his thesis, but I doubt that he used terms like "not substantiated" or "libelous." After all, this was the science of content analysis.

This newspaper and some of the popular magazines also liked stories about the illegal distillation of spirits or smuggling of same from Finland. The Finns seemed to be the underclass of Swedish society, right down there with other immigrant labor, but more firmly entrenched, over a longer period due to their proximity.

I had only a couple of fares that engaged in outright insult, both from Östermalm. One surly character wanted to go to Slussen to buy vodka late at night after the liquor stores closed. I knew nothing about this black-market trade and was told I should learn what driving a taxi was all about. Another was looking for a woman and acted incredulous when he found I had no connections.

Most Swedes, I discovered, were informal. Many wanted to ride in the front seat and would chat you up. Many also detected an accent and wanted to practice their English, learned as a compulsory second language in school, displacing German after World War II.

Once, while buying smoked herring from a street vendor, a teenager overheard my accent and stopped me, wanting to discuss the meaning of a stanza from one of Bob Dylan's songs.

"Oh yes," he said, "we study different dialects. Many of our teachers come from Great Britain and we learn mostly the English accent, but many of us kids want to know about what is being said by others . . ."

In a country of only eight million people, it is foolish to try to translate all the medical textbooks into Swedish for those Swedes studying medicine. The introductory textbook to economics at the University of Stockholm was the same text (Samuelson) that I had studied at American University in Washington, DC.

On another occasion, I was driving a fare who directed me to the western tip of the island of Longholmen, looking across the water, south to the tip of Reimerholmen. It was three o'clock in the morning, and with the October misty pale light from streetlights, he could only see where the island's tip met the water. I sensed the presence of buildings across the water but saw only trees. The motor was running, and the heater was on. The fare in the back seat had rolled down his window while he smoked. He said he just wanted to watch as the tanker from Italy approached the liquor commission docking and handling facility with its cargo of bulk wine.

"There's a lot of money in wine," he said.

I never did see a ship, much less one full of wine, but after 15 minutes, the guy in the back seat seemed satisfied and asked to be dropped off at the Hornstull subway station near Liljeholmsbron.

On another very dark early morning, I took directions from a large and agitated man to an industrial area, somewhere near Nacka, through a chain link and barbed wire gate and down a steep ramp to a dock. An immense tanker was due to arrive with a load of crude oil. The man said that it was a secret when the tanker arrived and where the oil was stored, but he had to be there, that it was his duty to be there for the unloading, and he had to be there before it arrived. The next day, I couldn't quite remember where I had been or how I had found my way back to the city.

I quit working for Sture Carlson right before leaving to visit Canada in the summer of 1971. I had worked full-time for a year and a half and was tiring of the alternating shifts, six days a week.

Chapter Eight
Kayak Trip and Other Pleasant Dangers

LETTERS

30 January 1970[37]

I pondered first man's loneliness and concluded it stemmed largely from his safety. To operate so cleverly in open space is a clear advantage, with no adversaries striking from the dark corners as in the days when we were propelled along by the instinctual motion of our spines in the primordial brine. It matters little if his God is a remnant of such danger or a rational precaution. The problem is so thoroughly confused by now that almost no one is satisfied. Perhaps if things appeared less safe . . . which avoids the problem of reality.

It has just occurred to me, like a dull thud from away far, that most of our inventions are fantasies. A hand of spiritual power touches us when we detect the thinness of the membrane between us, on that point of passing illusion: closing one's eyes in the brush during a game of "stalk," giggling when she complains of the joint in the tent, Pisces curled around the flame.

(unsigned)

---

37 Bruce omitted salutations and signatures on his letters with increasing frequency.

19 March 1970

Dear Folks,

. . . Vacation? Drank too much (more than once a week by Swedish standards) and eating all that meat and grease gave us the smelly farts. Air was good and clean; new vistas for the eyeballs and lots of sunshine. Came back thinking more about how Sweden is uninhabitable for seven to eight months of the year. Crocuses are coming up in British Colombia! It's dirty and wet here, ick.

The big news is that we are planning a trip to Canada this summer. A friend wants us to deliver a VW bus to him on the west coast, and we could look Vancouver over all at the same time. Flying into Montreal from Copenhagen and heading out west doing the camping routine . . .

Parker S. has decided to come out of his hermitage and help with the taxi driving. Now begins his long battle with the bureaucrats: yes, I am healthy, yes, I am registered, yes, I am a good boy have been good and will be (how about would have been) for evermore and anon

(could have been) and I believe in the father
(should have been) in the sky, father in the land,

Authority.
(unsigned)

19 April 1970

Dear Alan,

Just a matter of note to the effect that:

1. Have been informed of your plans to register C.O. soon.

2. We are going to Canada in mid-August probably to stay. The legal, professional, and climatic situation looks good.

3. You are welcome to join us for any reason and any duration.

4. Vancouver is the chief city on the edge of one of the few habitable wildernesses left.

5. P.H., D.G., and J.K. may someday encounter. (Disregard this)

6. What's #7

7. The weather is fine

I remember the spring of my senior year. Goodbye to Joan and the beginning of a very long and unfruitful engagement with the US military. These days it is worth every effort to keep from raising your hand and friend's, domestic and foreign. Well, we just wanted to let you know that if you choose, your sanctuary can be provided for. Never seen the West, have you boy?

Our Love, Bruce & Rosemary

Alan, 2014

I had mentally wrestled with my involvement in the Vietnam conflict throughout college. The impending possibility of actually killing people in Vietnam sunk in during the spring before I graduated in 1970. Although my selective service lottery number (rather high at 213) wasn't called, a new draft year would soon begin. So, I asked several family friends from the Unitarian, Quaker, and Jewish faiths to write letters supporting my application for C.O., or Conscientious Objector, status.

At that time, local draft boards provided a government appeal agent to counsel young men facing conscription prior to the official draft board hearing. Mr. Fullerton, my agent, questioned me for over an hour—about Bruce and my parents, and my affiliations at Earlham. Twice he asked, "You wrote the letter your parents signed in your defense, didn't you?" For years I have had a distinct memory of Mr. Fullerton physically tossing me out of his office into the hall—my notes scattering like startled pigeon feathers. But, as I learned from notes I dug out of my deceased mother's trunk, the recollection was an emotional one. The following—less dramatic but more accurate—is taken from notes I wrote the day after my interview with Fullerton:

> . . . At the close of the interview, Mr. Fullerton looked at me with the same mocking smile I have mentioned before and said, "So, you think Gandhi was a pacifist?" He was referring to statements in my C.O. claim that I had been influenced by Gandhi's writings. I answered yes and that I thought Gandhi was a very strong leader who knew what he wanted, but never used violence to attain his ends. I tried to make the point that Gandhi practiced passive resistance—*satyagraha*—which is a dynamic form of resistance and not a violent one. Mr. Fullerton, however, seemed disinclined to listen. He left the room as I was explaining why I thought Gandhi was a pacifist. My explanation trailed off in the corridor as I followed him out . . . .

> Needless to say, my claim was rejected by the local draft board, but my lottery number never came up, and I was never called into service. After the trauma of Bruce's desertion, I was very relieved—as were my mother and father.

During his naval retirement, our father mined the family's history for noteworthy descendents. One distant ancestor, Samuel Huntington, was the Governor of Connecticut from 1786 to 1796. He was a signer of the Declaration of Independence in 1776, and President of the United States of America in Congress Assembled in 1781. Perhaps this genetic thread reveals why Bruce was so interested in politics. When I was 14 and Bruce 19, he said, "Did I ever tell you I was going to be secretary of state someday?" The Huntington name has been meticulously maintained: my father is Robert Huntington Proctor; Bruce's older brother is Daniel Huntington Proctor. Dan named one of his sons Benjamin Huntington Proctor.

During America's Civil War, our great-grandfather, Wilbur Huntington Proctor, lied about his age (he was 15; enlistment age was 16) and split with his coconspirator parents from Connecticut the $600 enlistment bounty the Union Army was paying. He carried a diary throughout the Civil War and later served in the Western Territories of Oregon, Washington Territory, and finally, Ft. Boise in Idaho Territory. As I mentioned before, his diary is now preserved for posterity at Yale University.

Legacy: the pride that outlives the proud.

John Proctor, a direct descendant, became notable in modern times when playwright Arthur Miller, based his play *The Crucible* on Proctor's life and death by hanging as a witch during the Salem witch trials of 1692. The factual Proctor, a fiery and successful farmer, did not attend church during this era of strict, puritanical ethos. He was accused by his young servant, Abigail Williams, of bewitching her. In her court deposition, she testified:

> . . . I have seen the apparition of John Proctor Sr. among the witches and he hath often tortured me by pinching me and biting me and choking me and pressing me on my stomach till the blood came out of my mouth . . .

In fact, Proctor did beat the young girl when she suffered from fits and convulsions to "thrash the devil out of her," as he put it. Recent research provides credible evidence that the convulsions and fits in Salem attributed to witchcraft among the population may have been caused by ingesting rye grain contaminated with rye mold: ergot fungus. In any case, Proctor confessed what he knew to be a lie to avoid being killed, and then he recanted his confession for the sake of his dignity—and perhaps his soul.

Like his ancestor, Bruce had two choices: conforming to a system he knew to be riddled with lies or opposing the misled status quo—and suffering the consequences. John Proctor's consequence was decisive and quick: he was hanged on August 19, 1692. The outcome of Bruce's decision was psychological and drawn-out: he was unable to be the catalyst for change he so passionately desired in his youth.

Arthur Miller, coincidently, visited our summer neighbor Eli Wallach and Anne Jackson in 1960 when Eli was making *The Misfits* with Marilyn Monroe and Clark Gable—both stars' last film. Miller and Monroe were married at the time. Eli offered Marilyn a ride in his speedboat and asked Bruce to captain the craft. Still in high heels, Eli and Miller carried the woman across Three Mile Harbor's stony beach to the boat where my brother waited. They took off at full throttle. Years later Bruce mentioned to me that, as the craft's bow pounded the whitecaps on the harbor, Marilyn leaned her head on his shoulder and asked, "Can we go back now?" I don't think he mentioned her request to anyone at the time. Bruce was disappointed at the brevity of their trip, and after anchoring, he disappeared into our cottage to play solitaire.

LETTERS

8 June 1970

Dear Folks,

. . . Summer has finally come out of Russia as they call the southeast. Today I lost my driver's license, but don't know where to find it; went looking for it but ended up lying in the sun with a friend from California/N. Africa/through Europe/Sweden/Israel, (Kibbutz, mining in the hills) now in Sweden again. D.G. has two years left on his passport.

Now I'm waiting for Rosemary to come home. Mom, you were right about 2216 S. Dinwiddie Street.[38] Used to know the phone number, but I've had so many since, including Social Security and 349-6009 (Rosemary's telephone #), I'd give military ID even to the enemy.

Starting to see lifestyles as extensions out of the womb. We may be stopping over in Paris on the way to Canada. In the meanwhile, I figure I'm clearing $1.75/hr. and living high on $.80 bottles of wine, friends all around the world coming to visit me . . . My mother-in-law's mother is also

---

38   Bruce's early boyhood home in Arlington, VA.

having visions these days; my dear parents are memories of previous lives, and D tells me that is wishful thinking. I agree. He asks when it is possible to tell when the world has gone into introversion . . .

Just got your letter from June 2. P.H. is visiting us here in mid-August. We don't know how long after that we'll be here. Maybe a week, maybe two; it partly depends on H. and L. who say they'll be in Paris by September 1. We plan to buy a 29–45-day excursion round-trip ticket with SAS, lowest price possible after mid-August. On that you are allowed one stop-over which could be Paris. So, it looks like September at the earliest, but right now we can't be definite even as to where we'll spend the first year! Starting to get involved in the legalities of the thing. Many unanswered questions. Perhaps better to get "landed" status in Ontario . . .

Love, Bruce

10 July 1970
Gotland[39]

Dear Folks,

This place is just like East Hampton but on a bigger scale. We are on the west coast, so the sunsets are quite beautiful at 9:15. No harbor, but a hundred miles of the Baltic to the mainland. There're no barnacles and only a little seaweed on a wide shelf that drops off quite suddenly, as does the land to the sea, for the bank here is three times the height (as in East Hampton), and in irregular steps reflecting the land's slow emergence from the sea following the retreat of the glaciers. The cliff wall is clay and fossils compacted into horizontal strata that encourage the precipitous nature of the cliff. Further north, you can walk to the "high cliff" along the cliff edge. The beach route is difficult due to the

---

39   An island off the southeast coast of Sweden.

large boulders encountered as one nears the point where the cliff is highest. Further south is the head of the cove where a steep road slopes diagonally along the bank down to the fishing shacks. Not much fishing goes on today out of there. The property hasn't been as extensively sub-divided as East Hampton; the property we're on would make about three Proctor lots. On it are a one-and-a-half-room house, a one-and-a-fourth-room shack, and a two-room shed. We have the shed, Peter and Ingrid have the shack, and Ingrid's grandparents have the house. Grandfather built the shed and shack in the late '40s, but bought the house and land in '45, right after the Germans sank the SS *Hansa* making its way to Visby with vacationers. A 20-foot clinker-built fishing boat is slowly rotting a bit from the shack, bought, says Gramps, for $1.00 by "the boys." The soil is rocky and the woods are pine. Peter and I cut down a dead pine that had fallen into another tree, cut it up, and split it for the wood stove, only to be informed by uncle not to interfere—that we were guests of nature. Rosemary said that with that attitude, you'd have woods but no people in the woods. Uncle owns a hunk of woods back from the cliff. Their house is a Spanish chateau that the previous owner, a masseur who immigrated to Hollywood in the 1920s, sent back plans for in inches, and the carpenters made it in centimeters, so it's a splendid place with lots of rooms but low doors, staircases, etc. Somewhere between a dollhouse and the real thing. Good food, wine, etc. Played Scrabble without a board or numbered letters. Have been sightseeing in the old walled town, seen all the ruins, drove down south to the point. Land there looks like the pictures I've seen of western Ireland. Strawberries are in season. Drinking beer, swatting flies and mosquitoes, swimming and relaxing . . .

Bruce

Bruce, 2008–2009

Peter and Ingrid were married in July 1968. That winter was their first together, not counting the weeks they had in Vienna. The next year they spent in Hemmastavik and the year following on Idungatan in Vasastan at the Israel Mission, a dying remnant of the wartime relief from Germany and occupied Europe, with its 25-year-old display of knickknacks from foreign lands and the house guests living in some time inversion.

The day they moved in, I met them out front and we unloaded the truck. The quantity of junk necessitated several dozen trips up three flights of stairs. Sitting on the floor in the empty living room to rest, we made sandwiches, and because I was so tired, I slipped and drew blood with the cheese slicer. It is not unusual for a Swede not to speak if he has nothing to say and perhaps it is this quality which gives the impression of depth. To be alone with your own thoughts past the boundary of social compulsiveness is a well-developed necessity. So, they flee the city on the weekends, save a lifetime to buy a cabin in the woods, are very proud of a supposed self-reliance which is vaguely associated with boats and agricultural origins. A fine self-portrait but as a drunk once put it to me, "The Swedes like to think they're Vikings, but they aren't," dragging out the negation with a slurred emphasis. Indeed, my unknown tutor was right. If any have those qualities, it is the women. They are the daughters of the liberated; unlike the States, it happened here in the 1920s and 1930s, and they are on the other side of that transition now. The men are often spoiled and stupid, and those who are not put on a hard, stern exterior which inevitably cracks under the internal contradictions. The spontaneous wit or a generous friend is vastly appreciated, being so unusual.

Ingrid was neither of these but a rarer person yet. She easily escaped my categories with her magnificent head of long red-blonde hair. Her mood could be distant and serene and then fleetingly transposed to curiosity. Some things are easily said: she was a vegetarian, a painter, close to her family and two sisters. Her serenity contrasted with Peter's worries and petty complaints which never seemed to penetrate her self-control. She seemed to hold the melody and base of their relationship with Peter somewhere off on the piccolo, and the largest unresolved mystery of her was her love for Peter.

That third year they had Amanda, the daughter. The summer she was pregnant, we four went to her family's cottage on Gotland south of Visby on the cliffs over the Baltic facing into the late sunsets in July, Ingrid posing glamour shots for Peter's camera with her swollen belly and bikini.

We enjoyed the small pleasures of a vacation by the sea. Peter and I took long walks down the beach and flew kites. Rosemary and I waded along the shore looking for bright, shiny stones and shells, digging toes into the sand and occasionally splashing, though it was cold. I, with my birthday goggles, swimming out to the steep drop-off where the bottom plunged from 10 feet in a jagged escarpment far out of sight, the water clear to 30 feet, feeling the cold swirling eddies and diving down losing orientation to return to the surface out of breath and the beginning of a tingle of fear and respect for the ocean. The cliff, in loose terraces, was mounted by a zigzag path to the edge where the wind foreshortened pines followed the taper back to the woods and the cabin. We were the guests of nature and nobody dared to clean up the brush. It lay where it fell, except for one dead, bare pine infested with spiderwebs in the middle of the path to the trash can, which I pushed over and dragged away.

We took a day trip to the south end of the island and wandered by the craggy shore there and over what could have easily been Irish heath, finally settling into a dip of grass back from the cliff edge over which the wind blew through your hair if you stood up, but calm sitting in the sun picking pebbles out of the grass. We picnicked there and fed odd bits to the gulls clustered on the rise downwind. To throw bits of bread straight into the air where they were caught by the wind and dragged back into the mouths of gulls passed the time and marked their pecking order. A big, old, ugly gull finally bullied the others away and we left him hungry for his effort.

LETTERS

29 July 1970

Alan . . .

No injunctions, no questions, no answers. Driving taxi and pondering my fate. May go cut wood down in Smaland with Peter H., Peter S., and Dave G., wonder if I could be a youth adviser or janitor in a Unitarian Church. Wonder where it all goes. Hash might be legalized in Denmark(?) . . . Rain and wind, low temps. Here; just like fall in DC. The Canadians say I must have a job before I go there. "Don't quit your job or sell your house before hearing from us," OK—super crunch. In a pinch, you're welcome here, but I really don't think you'd dig the vibes. I'll send you the recipe when I find it, and meanwhile listen to Mr. Natural. Hope there is a semblance of communication here.

Bruce

4 August 1970

Dear Mom and Dad,[40]

. . . Now we are off for another week of sitting in the sun (if the weather holds out). Peter H. has arrived from Japan, complete with a ying-yong-yang way of speaking (or however you characterize a Japanese accent), lots of funny mannerisms, and a beautiful Japanese scroll . . . He and Bruce went off hitchhiking and rang me this morning from the edge of the Hardanger Fjord.

They sounded like they were having a good time. They should be back in town tomorrow late, or early Wednesday, and then we will go off together.

40 Mom and Dad Proctor, from Rosemary.

We had a disappointing interview with the Canadians. They are having a rather bad recession/depression. That is with six to nine percent unemployed and hardest hit is Vancouver. We immediately changed our application to read Toronto. But the size of it is, they don't need any immigrants, and if Bruce can't line up a job, we can't get in. (Me—they didn't even read my application, the bastards.) We had a long go-around about discrimination as an official Canadian policy???? Bruce was super. Anyway, as a result, Bruce feels like we should postpone for a while, and I concur. He will be in touch with Don J. (is that the name of the fellow in Niagara? Do you have his address?) and see if he can get an assist that way. Otherwise, we must make a trip sometime, and I just don't know when. Obviously, we've been talking about making such a trip for quite some time, and I suppose in a way I'm the bolt that keeps getting stuck—I get so involved in my work. But I really do think the move would be the best thing for us—it's just a matter of getting going. Meanwhile, I think Bruce will look for another job here this fall . . . perhaps something connected with map-making.

Are you going to see my folks on their way one direction or the other? It seems such a long time since we've seen any of you. Anyway, lots of love,

Rosemary

23 August 1970

Dear Folks,

Peter arrived at the end of July and we spent several days looking around Stockholm. I can't get too excited over it after so many times, but Peter thought it was a beautiful city. I guess it is. We got the idea to go to Norway, since Peter wanted to see a fjord, so at noon on Friday we hitchhiked out. Made the border the first night and stayed at a *pensionat*.

Continuing to Oslo the next morning, we were able to catch the late afternoon train to Bergen. Fantastic to see the up-country again, and then come down into Voss and then out to the coast. Crashed at an old bible college converted into a seaman's lodging. Finding the country more spectacular than the city, we bussed out next morning to where the road hits Hardanger fjord. The rest of the day we wandered down the coast thinking we were in Ilium or Shangri-La but were brought low by the price of the *pensionat* and the atmosphere: British bourgeoisie. Lounging around in the sitting room waiting for dinner, card playing after dinner. We went for a walk and took a swim in the fjord . . . zap, zap. Next morning, we decided we were running out of money. So, we hitched and hiked and only got over on the ferry and a little further on than Kinsarvik. Slept on the ground and got two good rides that put us in Oslo by 6:00 p.m. No money for room so we took the night train to Karlstad, but ended up going to Stockholm, out of money but none the less for wear. Rested a day and went to Copenhagen with Rosemary. We bicycled around Copenhagen, went to Tivoli, the movies, and drank lots of beer. Generally had a good time and camped out. Peter caught a night boat for Germany and we came home. Rosemary has been relaxing; I worked half of last week. Yesterday, Peter S. and I hitched down to Nynashamn, but I'm now back to work. Fallish weather is already upon us, fast drifting clouds upon the water, red buff brick churches, wheat bouquets . . . . Jim is taking LSD and grooving the California redwoods. Peter sits. Bruce drives.

[unsigned]

[undated—September 1970?]

We finished moving, finally. We will be here for a year, and we hope for longer, although it is impossible to say now.

It's a bigger place, quieter, newer. We have a tub and hot water! We are also thinking about buying a car. Rags to riches! I'm still driving a taxi and find it quite satisfactory; one is on one's own, almost outside and moving around. You get to know the city quite well, the study of traffic flow, peak hours, and strange characters. The disadvantages are the night shift every other week when your friends are playing and you're working, and the six-day workweek. I'd like five days a week on the day shift, then I'd have it made. The more I listen to Dylan, the more I wonder. The guy I drive with has been at it six days a week for 45 years! So, I've been thinking about switching, but such things need to be arranged. Rosemary and I and Frank (her boss) drove out in the country over the weekend. I got smashed and Frank went swimming. We ran into some friends along the way. We got a postcard from Peter H. so he is not lost. The secret of cleaning up one's room is to be utterly ruthless and throw away, otherwise the relatives have to do it eventually when one dies and it causes guilty feelings . . .

[unsigned]

Bruce, 2008-2009

Rosemary and I met Peter and Ingrid Sedgwick a year before. Peter was an American and Ingrid was Swedish. They had met in Vienna and Peter had fallen in love and followed Ingrid back to Sweden, where they were married. They lived in a second-floor apartment overlooking a courtyard. They were the maintenance team for a compound of apartments and the Mariakapella church.

Peter tended the furnace and looked after plumbing and electrical problems. Ingrid kept the staircases clean and washed and the two of them locked the doors to the street at night and took out the garbage. For the summer of 1970, they wanted to take the whole summer as vacation, stay at Ingrid's parents' *stuga* outside of Stockholm, do some traveling, and not be tied down to daily maintenance. They asked me and Rosemary if we would live in their apartment and look after things in their absence. They assured us that the work was minimal; there would be no problems with the furnace in the summer and the stairs were easy to keep clean without the sand and slush of winter.

So, we moved in. The apartment was fully equipped and comfortable, the rent was free, but I had to be around in case problems arose (and none did that summer). The living room looked out over the courtyard, across to the church, which was really a large chapel that fronted on Idungatan in Vasastaden, a neighborhood north of downtown, near SIPRI, that consisted of five-story walk-up apartments of stone construction from the 1920s.

I learned that this church had taken on a special mission during World War II. It devoted itself to housing Jews who had escaped from the Nazi terror, mostly from occupied countries like Denmark, but also from Spain and elsewhere. The large basement under the chapel was filled with collapsible cots covered in canvas. The canvas was dusty and old. The ambiance was more like a museum than a place of worship. In its heyday during the war, all of the pews were removed, and cots filled the sanctuary from wall to wall. A large kitchen turned out meals.

But now, there were no Sunday services in the sanctuary or refugees sleeping, and there was no minister evident. Unlike a museum, there were never visitors and, except for the noise that filtered in from the street, it was silent. No children lived with the other apartments' inhabitants, many of whom did not appear to be in residence and were seldom seen and rarely heard from. I had been warned which ones were to be avoided as cranky. All were old and had some connection to the mission from long ago. Peter told me that the church was supported by one Sundays's offering per year of every state church in Sweden.

The Swedish Church is Lutheran, state supported, and has official duties as the keeper of vital statistics. About 2 percent of Swedes attend church and state subsidies are necessary to maintain the churches and their grounds, lovely places which can be seen in hamlets and towns throughout Sweden. I had attended services in several of these and had toured the cathedral in Uppsala, seat of the church's primate.

I met the mission's secretary, an elderly lady and the only visible member of anything like administration. She was friendly and showed me the office. She produced a quarterly newsletter that had a mailing list of about 150. She complained that almost 40 percent of the newsletters mailed were returned as undeliverable or, written across the address, "deceased." There appeared to be little of substance in the one-page newsletter. Perhaps the "powers that be" had accepted Peter's recommendation of me and Rosemary for the job because I, too, had escaped from war, not as a Jew, but as a refugee.

In such an atmosphere, I soon became bored and thought that I needed a project. So, I decided to make a kayak. I had made a kayak before and had spent many hours in one on Three Mile Harbor. I ordered a plan from Great Britain of a type used in the lowland estuaries and other protected waters. It was built up from a keel with jig-sawed plywood ribs and three-fourth-inch by half-inch stringers running from stem to stern and covered with canvas. When the construction was finished, the kayak was turned upside down, canvas applied and tacked in place, and then thoroughly wetted and painted with clear "dope" to make it waterproof. "Dope" is really what it is called, and it is the same method used on fabric-covered airplanes before the use of aluminum skins.

Construction took place in the chapel's basement boiler room, which was sometimes uncomfortably warm from the central hot water heater, even with the windows open. I was the only one who ever went to the boiler room; nobody else had reason to do so. It was the only space under cover that was big enough for the 16-foot boat. In addition, the end of the room had a large, operable window at ground level through which the completed boat could be removed. I did the doping outside in the courtyard since it is highly flammable and toxic. Breathing the fumes was not advised.

Now that I had a kayak, I wanted to try it out, so I began to plan a trip into the Skargarden. The kayak could be launched just behind Wenner-Gren Center, into Brunnsviken, a tongue of water that led, without having to make a portage, into Stockholm's harbor, connecting to channels through the Skargarden to the Baltic Sea further east. My goal was to paddle to Nynashamn at the southernmost edge of the Skargarden. I judged that the waters were protected enough for this to be safe, even though Rosemary was worried because I would make the trip alone, close to 60 miles through largely unin-habited waters. I was not worried; I was a strong swimmer and had been a Red Cross–certified lifeguard in high school.

Bert supplied me with nautical charts that, by dead reckoning, would guide me out of the channels of Stockholm harbor, east into the Skargarden. Bert pointed out the main shipping channels that were to be avoided in favor of the smaller leads east and then south-east to my destination.

Dead reckoning presumes a sense of scale . . . read the map . . . gauge your distance between point A and point B . . . no need for a compass . . . just orient yourself in the direction of travel. I had the nautical charts in clear waterproof bags. I had the maps in my lap as I paddled east.

The first day out of Stockholm, through Stockholm's harbor, I passed many landmarks that could not be seen from the roads—the veterinary hospital—the narrow lead from Brunnsviken out into the oil-soaked waters of Stockholm's harbor and then on through the channels north of Lidingö. I paddled and paddled some more. It was August, the water was not warm, and I controlled the drip off of my double-bladed paddle the best I could so that the cold water would not dribble down my arms. By late afternoon, I was beginning to fatigue. Although I had tried to prepare through exercises, after hours of paddling, I was sore and tired—way beyond the city and habitation by late afternoon. I could camp anywhere.

I chose a spot in the lee of a small island. The surface of the water was clear and unbroken as I came up to the spot I had seen, in the failing light. Slowly, I nosed the kayak onto the sandy shore. Slower still I disembarked, cautious not to become wetter than I was.

Carefully, I prepared the fire that would warm me, dry out my wet gear, cook my supper, and provide enough warmth for a restful night in a dry sleeping bag, here, east of the city in a wilderness of water, rock, trees, and islands.

I consulted Bert's map. I was on schedule. Rosemary was to meet me in three days. No problem. I slept well and, upon arising after a quick *smorgos* breakfast, set out again, the relentless paddling, the dead reckoning, further east down the channels, staying to the lee side of the land.

Luckily, there was no rain; lucky for August, as this was not always the case. At midday, I rounded the point of an island, and gazing up onto a slope of clean rock facing to the south, I saw a young woman, sunbathing on the rocks, stark naked, absorbing the warmth of the sun and the warmth of the rock. I silenced my paddles, slipped through the water like an Algonquin warrior on full alert, not to disturb the scenery, much less the ambience of my own voyeuristic pleasure. She never saw me—was never disturbed in whatever reverie she was in—neither was I, sliding through the water, past her, out of sight, the sun now at my back.

Certainly, this is a magic place, I thought, *wherever else, whenever else . . . however else . . . could I be blessed with such majesty . . . of the spirit . . . of the senses . . . what has brought me here . . . why am I so lucky?*

But then I misread the chart and turned south down a blind bay, thinking I had found the channel to Kanalaren Dalaro. This was a mistake that cost me an hour of paddling to get back on course. Exhausted, I arrived at Dalaro canal. The campsite and amenities were good. I bought some fresh smoked herring and had *smorgosar* from my pack for supper. I made camp and fell into the tent and warm, dry bag. I awoke early in the morning to yet another clear day—and still no rain—God bless!

South of the Dalaro canal, the archipelago opened up into a seemingly vast stretch of islands, thin in their east/west direction and long to the north/south. On the third day out, I was now headed due south to Nynäshamn. These islands had a fascination. Sometimes they were only 30 feet across, but half a mile long, north to south, like the spine of some fantastic serpent, immobile . . . treacherous, yet sublime in their soft surrender . . . solemn in their watery silence, spiky spines towering over my head as I was pushed south on the following wind, close to the ragged shoreline.

Sometimes, I would see submerged rocks sliding by and think, *how far to the nearest land if one of these rocks rips this canvas, stem to stern . . . or, even a big tear.* I had not seen a single boat all day . . . there were no houses or cabins in sight. *I'm glad I brought the canvas repair kit,* I thought, although I had never used it. *This would be perfect for sailing and I'd make good time on the long run down to Nynäshamn. I have only come halfway and I'm supposed to meet Rosemary tomorrow morning . . .*

I had twine and a poncho, but nothing to hold up a jury-rigged sail. I studied the shoreline for driftwood and pulled in at a small cove where debris had accumulated on the lee side, found two poles from among the deadfall on shore, and lashed them together, forming an *X*. Then I lashed the square poncho to it, hood down so the drawstrings could be used to storm-rig the sail, and then fastened sheets to the bottom two corners of the poncho. With the *X* in front of me at deck-height, I pushed off from shore, tentatively, into the sheltered breeze.

My thoughts focused on the inherent danger: *I must be careful—the wind could easily tip me over—and I need both hands on the paddle for a rudder—there is just a thin layer of canvas with dope between me and this cold water.*

As I settled into the back of the cockpit, my life-preserver acting as a backrest and tethered to my belt, sitting on the floorboards that rested on the keel, the port and starboard sheets tucked between my thighs and the gunnels, the driftwood lower ends cushioned with rags so they wouldn't punch through the thin skin, my bare toes holding the branches against the mid-ship rib, I began the balancing act that this rig required. I saw the poncho begin to flutter in front of me, obstructing the view forward, making it difficult to see any submerged rocks that could rip the boat's skin. I headed out into the main blow of the north wind, away from shore rocks, I hoped. But out in the main channel I'd also be further from land. If I tipped over into the cold, August water . . .

The waves were just beginning to white-cap, but I was soon cutting through them with curls cut from my bow, sometimes cascading over the foredeck as I mastered the balance and let out the sheets on the bottom of the poncho so that it rose above the deck like a true spinnaker, allowing a clear view forward for any rocks.

With the long, double-bladed paddle firmly anchored by my right hand to the gunwale and the blade extended back under the keel for good steering leverage, the pressure on my arms was challenging, leaving risky options for trimming the sheets by hand while holding the mast with my toes and balancing the boat with shifts in my body.

At one point, gazing east, I saw what I thought was a destroyer, no doubt a Swedish warship . . . up against an island far to the east

. . . and what looked like a hardened bunker or slip within the granite heart of the island . . . a hardened site in anticipation of some holocaust from the east.

I had read *The Hobbit* and *The Fellowship of the Ring* and imagined myself as a seafaring Hobbit, careening along the border of Mordor, dancing on the wind, below any radar detection and close enough to islands to go unseen from a distance as anything but driftwood.

Later, I learned that some of the Jews escaping from Denmark across the Öresund, in their desperation, after having missed earlier opportunities by ferry, yacht, and boat, had escaped by kayak.

As late evening approached, the wind dropped, I abandoned my driftwood masts on the shoreline, and for the first time that day, I had to paddle—through the harbor at Nynäshamn and beyond, following the shoreline to the peninsula campground, which was deserted. I picked the prime campsite which gave views north up the channel and south across a large placid bay dotted with islands. I made a fire, cooked a meal, and crawled into my sleeping bag, gazing out to the southwest as twilight enshrouded.

I awoke to a cool clear morning, the sun rose by five, but I was reluctant to leave the warmth of my sleeping bag. The previous day's north winds had cooled the weather, but the wind was timid. I knew that I had little to eat and nothing to do but wait for Rosemary. I was glad that I did not have to get back in the kayak and into the cold water. Finally, nature called, and I emerged from my cocoon and took a walk around the peninsula campground, still deserted. I found the road out, but there was no sign of life and not even the birds were stirring. I returned to my camp, spread out my wet gear in the sunlight, made coffee, and devoured my remaining morsels of flatbread, salami, and cheese. I was still hungry, but there was nothing to do but wait.

By midmorning, Rosemary showed up with Connie's VW Bug and roof rack, saying, "I thought I'd never find you." I was very glad that she did. A 16-foot kayak upside down on the roof of a Beetle makes a strange sight, as if you could flip it over and ferry the Bug across the water. We headed toward Nynäshamn along a narrow coastal road that turned around the headlands and twisted over the ravines, with nice views of the water; I was happy to see them from somewhere else than sea level, the views constantly changing without having to paddle.

Rosemary described in detail her difficulties in finding me, this road being her last, desperate attempt. I was glad to listen to another human voice, her voice. Then stories and gossip since when I had left. It seemed like more than three days.

We had lunch in Nynäshamn and I began to relax as we headed back to Stockholm. I felt that I must have lost some weight and left some other things behind as well.

LETTERS

[undated—probably September or October 1970]

. . . We hope Mother is learning to take it a bit slower. We worry about her/you, Mother. Even we are feeling older these days and Bruce has quit working full-time. He drives two to three times a week and is discovering the art of reading and sitting without going crazy. The Social Democrats are still in power here after a close election. The big debate now is over joining the E.E.C.

Whether or not they travel the road to integration now or later seems irrelevant, for to me, I see it inevitable that the world will have a fully integrated labor/capital/resource market and eventually a social democracy which guarantees the objects of existence in equal proportion to the inhabitants of the planet. Without it, "the meaning of man" is a hopelessly hypocritical search for insubstantial values. Whatever that's worth.

R.

Alan, 2014

In the summer of 1970 after graduating from Earlham, our harbor cottage was being rented and I was house-sitting and doing minor repairs to the cabin next door to ours. In the evenings, I performed my own songs at the Stephen Talkhouse in Amagansett and the Grotto of the Purple Grape—a Bridgehampton bar. The artist Andy Warhol came into the Grotto one evening with six of his groupies—all young women. I chose my first song carefully: "The Ballad of Shaggy Joe," about the tentative life of the artist—or, for that matter, about the tentative life of the exile. The song's last line is, "There are no more donut holes like Shaggy used to make." Warhol seemed totally stoned; he didn't leave a tip which infuriated the waitstaff.

I occasionally heard from Bruce by letter; my life was also on a kind of "hold." I had no real job prospects and no place to go but home. A young woman acquaintance from college visited me while I house-sat. She teased me mercilessly by traipsing around the house topless. No touchy-touchy . . . she had a boyfriend. The owner of the cottage found out she was staying with me and threw us out. That same day I got a call from my father who told me mother had been diagnosed with bladder cancer, what Rosemary was referring to when she wrote, "We hope Mother is learning to take it a bit slower. We worry about her/you, Mother." My visitor went home, and I spent that night huddled in a sleeping bag in the yard. The next day I drove to Oklahoma.

Chapter Nine
Yoga, Booze, and Dope

LETTERS

October 1970

Dear Carol, Joe, Mark, and Joey [Kozlevcar],

Fall is upon us here and we're still in Stockholm. I don't understand it. I am driving taxi, but only two days a week, and I can study Swedish and keep my head from rotting. Rosemary is busier than ever with her editing work. She's carrying the chief editorial load for three books a year now. I remember some of those government editors at DOD[41] who did a book's worth every three years. The monetary unit here is the crown. One crown, two crowns, three crowns which is beer. As to whether Bruce will be teaching in Canada, who knows. As I said, I don't understand it. If we tell you all our plans, there'll be no surprises for anybody. In the meantime, I'll wait on events. Is Nixon really going to stop the war? Is the US economy really recovering? Does it really concern us? Well, no more answers. Just keep eating, breathing and lovin' one 'nother.

Bruce & Rosemary

---

41   Department of Defense.

27 October 1970

Dear Alan,

. . . I think that we'll be in Canada in May–June of '71, at least that's what Rosemary is saying at this point. She hasn't seen her parents for over two years and thinks it's about time. We'll probably come over on the 45-day tour. Frankly, it would have to be a pretty good offer to get me to stay over there. Here, I work a two-day week, and manage to support my end of the household. Otherwise, I go to two classes a week to learn Swedish, a project I never seem to get my head into completely because I have yet to hear anything interesting said in Swedish. Surprised? No, I guess not, you've been here and caught the creeping death vibrations.

I'm getting back into shape with my hatha yoga and trying to launch into laya yoga. Quite a routine: internal cleansing, vegetarian diet, sitting, gazing, concentration, and mantra. Oh well, someday soon maybe. Up until recently, was doing the dope pretty heavy. Back in August when Peter was here, had a piece spiked with opium. Strange shit! You start hearing someone working with a wrench two blocks away. Your mind just kind of spreads out. Before that a piece of really fine hash. Before that, was growing my own grass like last summer. After Peter was here, scored a big piece of Moroccan Kief. Pretty good, but all the time coming down, grainy eyeballs, getting nowhere, and spirit low; could have been bad but for the old patience. Screw that and went to drinking; about the same sort of routine, but better in some ways not as good in others . . . the head snobbism about alcohol is just that . . . so now I'm just sitting around making no apologies, reading *The Electric Kool-Aid Acid Test* and trying to figure it all out . . . like I knew it all by the grapevine, the synch, Jung, *I Ching*, Cassidy, Owsley. An incredibly open fellowship communicated by letter and mouth; is it still alive? I doubt it in the old form anyway; all is underground these days, everybody hiding, maintaining coolness . . . seriously, don't play the bastards' game! The more I learn about Sweden, the happier I am that I didn't grow up here, and glad to be a guest, *Tack* for *det*. Funny thing is, just sitting here pounding out this letter makes me feel better, like renewing the old cosmic brotherhood, making something of the space in-between: highways, apartment buildings, ownership, grind, twaaang, thwap, like when the outside mic breaks off the Prankster's bus and hits the pavement at 60 mph, fully amplified to everybody within, and Cassidy at the wheel.

Sometime in November, Rosemary and I plan to go down to Paris for a couple of weeks, and I'm thinking about spending some time on the Moroccan beaches. They say you can live down there for 20 cents a day. Like, work three months in Sweden and . . . Rosemary always figures into these things, career . . . hmmmmmmmmm. Off to study Swedish and eat lunch. Send me your new address so I don't have to mail this through the parents. Like, they can open it up and discover their son is a dope fiend. Sure folks, have a toke. I do miss that old Mexican grass, giggles, smile, and all so light and gay. Damn hash is like a sledgehammer, shut-up and listen, kid!

[unsigned]

Alan, 2014

Like many of my generation, I smoked a lot of marijuana on weekends during college. When I traveled to London to study English during my junior year abroad, my roommate scored a potent chunk of hashish, its dark brown square the size of a matchbox and texture of tar. Lew sliced thin, aromatic slivers into our shared pipe. He handled the drug with a delicacy that reminded me of baiting a very sharp hook. I could relate to Bruce's assessment of the stuff: "shut up and listen, kid" indeed . . . to the street noise heightened into a kind of mechanical chant by the drug, to the Westminster chimes exploding like M-80s downstairs in our landlady's hall. It is interesting to note that, according to *Webster's New World Dictionary*, the word "assassin" is derived from the word "hashish." Senses heightened and directed into a killing rage by scheming masters? Bruce must have had a high tolerance for his on-again, off-again binges with drugs and alcohol. Even under the influence, he always seemed rock-solid to me; he giggled occasionally—private jokes from some mind-ether. When my girlfriend and I visited him in Stockholm, I remember sitting in a garden reading a book with Bruce meditating right next to me in a lotus pose. When I looked up at the chapter break, he was standing on his head—perfectly still. My peripheral vision hadn't caught any movement. At another chapter break when I glanced up, he was on his back, feet extended behind his head, arms splayed in the opposite direction on the ground—the plough posture. His mastery of yoga was astounding.

LETTERS

3 November 1970

My friend Peter has learned many things. I must tell him that, once in the States, yes, we did hitchhike together to NY (to Dobbs Ferry from Washington) and I was sworn to secrecy about it because Marion didn't like Peter hitching. She is a clever woman and managed to learn the truth by cross-examining me. Peter felt betrayed, and I was sorry to the point of suppressing the entire episode even until his question this summer, "Have we hitchhiked together?"

Last week I recommenced my yogic routine with specific exercises on Monday, Tuesday, Thursday, and Friday mornings for the abdomen, plan one and general exercise on the same afternoons, light form plan one with additions of my own. Last week I was doing eight repetitions. This week I'm doing 10. The following yoga exercise plans followed some of those contained in *Hatha-Yoga* by Professor Shyam Sundar Goswami, L.N. Fowler & Co., Ltd., second edition.

Last week the morning schedule was: Dynamic Abdominal Posture Exercise Plan one, Modified Both-nostrils Breath Control Exercise with Abdomen relaxed 15–20 times.

Spine Posture	10 times
Spine Posture with hands clasped behind head	10 times
(couldn't do so substituted spine posture)	
Plough Posture	10 times
Sideward Leg-Motion Posture	10 times
Head-Knee Spine Posture	10 times
Bow Posture	10 times
Boat Posture	10 times
Modified Both-Nostrils Breath Control	15-20 times

The afternoon schedule was general exercise, light form, plan one with additions:

Modified Both-Nostrils Breath Control Exercise	15-20 times
Neck Flexion-Extension	8 times
Neck Rotation	8 times
Toe Posture	8 times
Thigh Posture	15 times
Serpent Posture	8 times
Modified Locust Posture	8 times
Back-Stretch Posture	8 times
Spine Posture	8 times
Head-Knee Spine Posture	8 times
Plough Posture	8 times
Sideward Leg-Motion	8 times
Pelvis-Raise Posture	8 times
Crows-Head Posture	1 time
Single Foot-Head Posture	8 times
Risen Lotus	8 times
Arm Motion	8 times
Quadruped Posture	14 times
Shoulder Posture	
Modified Both-Nostrils Breath Control	15-20 times

Exercises with Abdomen relaxed Additions were made for abdominal and pectoral limb areas.

This week I'm doing 10 repetitions morning and night. Changes from the above schedule are:

1. Can now execute several Spine Postures with hands clasped behind head;

2. Head and knee actually touch in Head-Knee Spine Posture;

3. Breathing now consistently at 20 times;
4. For afternoon: do Abdominal-short-quick breath-act before and after exercise, three rounds 30 times each; do 16 quadruped posture; do Head Posture for three minutes.

3 November 1970

Dear Folks,

I have just finished dinner and my yoga and spending a "quiet evening at home." Rosemary went to her statistics class and then will go to a wine party at the assistant director's house to celebrate the publication of the second yearbook which she edited. I headed off to drive taxi this morning, but the taxi I had reserved wasn't there, so I bicycled home again; that was somewhat tricky due to ice on the roads; it's getting quite cold now. I bought myself a new heavy coat and fur hat. I am driving two to three days a week and I find that it fits my endurance and the needs of the household. I use the rest of the time in reading and doing yoga.

Apropos Mother's remark about Spiro Agnew, have you seen him in "Pogo"? I have been thinking about going back to the university, but I don't know if I'm ready for it; I just may wait several years. When it comes to Canada, we had a report from Jim in Seattle that the mayor of Vancouver was considering using the emergency war powers to get rid of all the "hippies, deserters, and bums." Who needs it? Things are smooth and easy here; and I'm beginning to enjoy being a European; simply living and enjoying, no guilt about suppressed minorities, crisis, etc., life grinds on. Plenty of time to do my thing. No Halloween here; call it All Saints Day, a vacation, visit the graveyard, visit the relatives, drink too much, and get killed on the highway syndrome . . .

Saturday night we had a poker party with a group of friends. Sunday, we went to the movies. We've been seeing quite a few old ones of the social protest genres from old USA 1930s. Ever seen any of these documentaries? *And So They Live; People of the Cumberland; The Inheritance; The Plow that Broke the Plains; The River; Valley Town; The City; The Heart of Spain; The Wave; Native Land; Metropolis.* Both Willard Van Dyke and Paul Strand came to comment on their films. In all it was a great study of the '30s from the then radical reform perspective. Pete Seeger singing union songs, the heavy stress on "our American rights," the pioneer spirit "we are strong" thing, and the hope in the efficacy of union. Too bad every generation has to do it all over again. Films were presented by the Worker's Education Alliance. Too bad Americans are stuck with their constitutional system. Perhaps a responsible party system would end some myths about America. Always good to be disillusioned.

Our love, Bruce & R.

4 November 1970—Wednesday

Walked home from Sveavagen 122 at 1600 through the crisp leaves, crackling ice-covered from the light snow and sleet. Over Hoga and through Norra Begravingsplats, a dark early evening between the graves to Margit, Petit, and Oscar, a towering headstone with elaborate runes. Headed northwest to the Solnavagen fence where I could find no gate and followed the path along the fence to the crematorium and then over the *torp* and on the south flank, the mausoleums in their great squat bulks of gray granite, the burnt-out candles on their thresholds testimony to poor housekeeping. But no gate on the industrial area, the main railroad line north and west out of the capital city, or *Huvudsta*, my home. Death it seems had turned its back on modern life and intercepted me in its maze.

[unsigned]

15 November 1970

Tuesday morning's yoga pinched a muscle in the right side of my lower back, so I didn't do Tuesday afternoon. Started again on Thursday, but Friday morning was only sun salutations, and in the evening, Dave came home with news of having gotten "asylum," so we drank wine.

Smoking Tuesday and Wednesday beer on Thursday. Saturday help-day. Saturdaynight went to Ostgok for pizza and then to theater to check on *Catch-22*; they had sold our reserve tickets. As a result, decided to maintain last week's schedule with a repetition increase of one. Think back trouble came from doing heavy back exercise on Monday afternoon, i.e., snake and locust. Probably too radical an increase from the serpent, modified locust, which I was doing previous week. Just like Goswami said: increase repetitions slowly and build up to high repetitions before switching to heavier contractions! Future planning starts at home.

[unsigned]

17 December 1970

Dear Family [Kozlevcars],

Something for Joey and Mark is on its way air and should reach you before Christmas. Something for Joe and Carol is on its way surface and probably won't get there till the middle of January. If it's broken, you can't feel guilty or you'll have to confess it (my rule). Recently turned down a job offer with IBM because I'd have to travel to the States. Oh well, the American Empire strikes back! Rosemary's folks are coming at the end of the month, and we are both cleaning house. Dave has moved out in celebration of his acceptance in Swedish Society. Bruce and Rosemary announce their coming visit to Canada in the early summer of '71. Your last chance to see them before the amnesty.

Bruce and Rosemary

January 1971

Dear Alan,

Just been working on my income tax for 1970 and discovered that I cleared $2,400 US for driving taxi six days/week February–September. Seems silly to work in the summer and lie around in the winter, so I'm applying for my scholarship on the general philosophy of "take it while you can get it . . ." Have been thinking about the impossibility of taking Zen vows. Scored 22 grams of Turkish for $20, wow! Am sitting here drinking wine and smoking. Had a fog relapse which started at a Christmas Day party, so much good booze (champagne cocktails yet). Also, haven't been doing much yoga since before Christmas; gads, before Paris. Now, when I get the urge to move, sometimes I end up in a lotus, sometimes in the fish posture which guarantees instant enlightenment whenever you need it. Have also started Swedish again so I can stay current with their freshman requirements . . . Just took a long break to do *heian* No. 4, an old karate form. Have you ever seen any films of old Chinamen doing forms in the Peking Parks?

I was led to a good billiard hall here. Not my game. Have I seen any films? Saw *2001* again and remembered we had a big conversation once, seems you maintained Hal was behaving rationally; like leave well enough alone. Like spending half a year's wages to go on vacation. Your running around (New Mexico and Texas) sounds terribly adventurous to us. Eight hours drive from here is Copenhagen, and that seems like a long way. I remember driving through the Texas panhandle one February. We left Oklahoma City in the afternoon in my VW Bug and hit the panhandle and a snow storm at dusk. The snow (and we) continued all night long in third gear. Over Raton Pass the snow stopped, and the sun came up as we hit Pueblo. Glaze ice was two inches thick on the road, and we slid right into the central ditch of a deserted interstate highway after doing a slow 360-degree spin. No control at all. It was a little tricky getting out of there.

[unsigned]

5 March 1971

Dear Folks,

I am sitting at Rosemary's typewriter at work with nobody around, so the inclination hit me to discourse. The hottest thing around is a revolt of the workers of SIPRI, mainly the researchers but also most of the support personnel. It seems that everybody is getting to resent the director's procedures. They can't demand that their versions of manuscripts be accepted since only the director has that power by law (law?). One researcher has resigned, and the others have submitted a memo on these problems. A simple innocent memo and Rosemary thinks it might mean her job. She's been working a six- and seven-day week for 14 hours a day . . .

We have a very old VW Bug borrowed from a woman at SIPRI, who is on vacation for two weeks, and I've already had to rescue the thing three times, it overheats and quits.

Mike and I took it out toward the Skargarden, and it died on us; the next day we rescued it, and on the third day we took a bus instead out to the boat, an old low-decked archipelago cruiser, out to Namdo, first populated by German monks. The boat went into a landing that hadn't been opened all winter, slowing through 15 centimeters of ice into the bay, and finally stopping, backing, and trying again. It took three tries to make it. Then we cut overland to a little shack that Mike had used in November when he was lumbering. The place was being used so that eliminated Rosemary and my plans to come out there for a week over Easter. Patches of snow are still on the ground out in the country and the ground is wet underfoot like the sloshing farmers in Sandburg poems, rubber knee-high boots the only protection against the all-permeating damp. I had on my leather combat boots and got them thoroughly soaked. We beat it back to the boat landing and had a glorious 10 minutes on the dock sunning ourselves although it was cool enough for winter jackets. The only sound was the melting of water and the wind in the trees. Ten minutes away from the mechanical grind of civilization. "Well," I reflected on the dock, "if the boat doesn't come, we have three sandwiches and can go back to the cabin for the night. No question about survival."

"Yes," added Mike, "so let's go back to the city where there is a challenge . . ."

[Letter to be continued.]

Bruce, 2008–2009

So, Mike and I headed out toward Stavsnäs on the Värmdö road in Connie's '58 VW Bug. It was an early spring day, cloudy gray landscape slipped by the windows of the car. On the road to Gustavsberg and beyond, patches of snow were left in the ditches and on the shade side of woods and rock outcroppings. Mike had been cutting timber on Namdo the previous October in the rain and lowering clouds of a late autumn. We were on our way there to pick up some things he had left in a cabin on the north side of the island. We had almost gotten to Stavnas when we came over a rise in the road and noticed that we were right behind the bus that was going there when the VW died. It just stopped running. We got out and took a look. Turning it around on the hill, we tried to jump-start it going in the other direction. No luck. Neither one of us felt like bothering with it, so we locked up and stuck out our thumbs. Perhaps it was the third car, a new sedan that stopped. Mike climbed in the back and I next to the driver, a mature guy, gray on the temples, in colorful sport clothes. "Thanks a lot," we said in Swedish.

"We've gotta help one another," he said.

As Mike observed later, the cat was right on. And so were we, right into Medborgarplatsen and the subway station, sailing the whole way, this cat driving like most Europeans in a new car, what the car, the road, and the law, if you saw him, permitted. Back into town on the old yo-yo.

Feeling generally anti-climaxed by the turn of events, we broke out Mike's smoked ham sandwich and my sandwiches and a beer which we proceeded to wolf and guzzle on the platform of the station and into the subway car amidst the rush-hour gawking of Swedes who were hungry and abashed by these ill-mannered miscreants. "Good beer," Mike said. So, through the depths of Central Station and out the other side to Östermalmstorg we rode, chewing and swigging, the wail of wheels competing with the doodley-bop in our brains. Östermalm is Mike's neighborhood, and he led the way directly to Stockholm's best pub on Grevgatan. It was nearly empty, and we quickly settled into Guinness draught, one, two, and three big ones. Soon it was creeping up our spines and the English bartender feeding Woodstock tunes into the cartridge tape recorder giving the whole thing the old four-time bump. Mike was on about adventures in the Poconos, height of the season, working in the kitchen of this big place with receptions and drunken parties, him in his serving whites drinking it up and finally in a stupor sinking into a chair, rapping with some guy who finally says, "You're drunk," and proceeds to slop him across the front with a full bottle of ketchup. Both of us sinking back to dig the dart game and the recently arrived chicks and just-out-of-work businessmen in their suits and broad ties, tweeds and long blonde hair in the heart of this closed-at-11:00, police-station-around-the-corner neighborhood, bar: up from the docks, on the hill, in the spring . . . And this one chick talking how it's a great job to this friend who joined her (after we joined her, after a few at the bar), hello to the guys she knew, kidding all around: about how she comes into the office at noon and here it is six. By this time, we're on shots of straight whiskey.

Finally, out into the street and on up into the neighborhood to a good pool hall Mike knows though it's exclusive, and we walk right in because the control is not functioning or something, I don't understand, and so on to the lousiest shooting we've both ever done. I catch a bus and walk up to Wenner-Gren Center, stand beneath the sixth-floor window and yell for my Rosemary. No face, no lights, really, except for the middle of the fifth floor. No phone around, so I look for a taxi at Sveaplan, find one and am back at Mike's place. He's hardly surprised to see me, and it seems a party is shaping up. I call Rosemary; she is tired and disappointed that I didn't call earlier. I hit the road home, out to Solna on the bus.

Thursday morning, I borrow Karin's car and pick up Mike to rescue Connie's car. Things are already strange. Out past Gustavsberg once more and we find the car in the ditch with a parking ticket. It starts right up, and I lead the way back at a limping pace, stopping to change oil; the problem seems to be overheating. By the time we hit Stockholm, she's really hot, but we make it to Wenner-Gren Center without its quitting. We park by Haga Park, come in the back way and take the strange corridor to the main lobby. Cut-out geometric shapes protrude out of the right-hand wall; indirect lighting projects weird patterns on the left-hand brick wall. The corridor takes a right and a left, and at the end are a dozen or more foot-wide pipes from floor to ceiling. Making a final left, we see the stillness of the green carpeted lower foyer. After dropping off the keys, we head back to Mike's place and have coffee and bread with Lisa and her sister. I am once more rapt in wonder at the beauty of spoken Swedish; its melodic rise in midsentence, the round vowels drawing emotions. Another party is shaping up, but I head back to pick up Rosemary.

Friday morning, Rosemary and I pick up Mike and his pack to try once more for Namdo. Down to the Borgmastargatan bus station where Rosemary drops us off. We're taking no chances this time. We get our safe bus connection and out on the road to Stavsnas. Mike muses on ways of city folk and their general lack of sympathy for what is going on around them, like a country type would say, "wow, what's happening here," and they would all put their heads back into their papers thinking, "Oh, one of them!" Little kids are along the road goofing on the way to school. The *Norrskär* is moored at Stavsnas pier. She's an old archipelago boat of wide beam and low decks. The upper deck is fitted with a dining room, formal sitting room, and a smoking room aft of the central ladder. We stow our packs and wander into the dining room, empty but for the platinum-blonde matron with two dogs in a carrying bag. Her jowls are tanned, and their slight sag gives her that distain which would be class elsewhere. There's nobody else around, so I end up in the little galley, look in the cooler and see it's packed with Stenbock, so I take a couple and rummage through a drawer for the opener. Glasses from the cabinet and we're set. Mike starts the story of how he came to be here.

"I was working the cats on the *Enterprise* with John and Rick; deck work, a crummy job, but it was nice with your friends around. We fucked off too much as we always did, and I got sent around to arresting gear. They thought we were new on board, so they spent all this time showing us around. Of course, we didn't say anything except ask dumb questions like where's the mess hall, huh . . . Boy, were those guys mad when they found out. They'd have these drills, security, when everybody would have to go somewhere and hope there wasn't somebody there who didn't belong. The buzzer would go and suddenly people are dashing madly down the passageway knocking you over if you're in the way. Crazy. What a big ship. We were in a storm in the Atlantic (was it? Yes, it must have been between the Mediterranean and Norfolk) and you could walk on the walls, and the whole thing corkscrewing so that whole racks of dishes would go crashing onto the decks and slide against the opposite bulkhead. That was bad, but worse yet was the three-day boat ride to Russia."

He lost me there, so I got it straightened out that he was on leave in Tokyo with Rick, John, and Craig when they talked to this chick who dug their situation and put them on to Behren and a Zen Buddhist monk who said they should see the Russians. So, they went to the embassy and they said there was nothing they could do, but if they happened to be on the Russian boat leaving Japan on the morning of X from Z, and they weren't apprehended in the meantime by the harbor police and passed customs, then they might see them in Russia. So that put them on the boat to Russia . . .

The waiter came in the middle of all this, did his uptight gig about how we got served, and we paid him.

It was an exceptionally clear day, the bright sun sparkling off the unmelted snow and the water, the clear, dark blue Baltic, ice-free in the deep channels. The archipelago in the early spring; ice in the bays and passages, snow on the north face of the tear-drop islands dotting the sea, the large ones blocking the horizon with pine stands. The channel to Namdo became littered with floe ice as we plied between unbroken sheets. We left the channel and began to cut into the ice toward Namdo. The boat went slower, and the old diesels rattled her as they strained against ice . . . As we cut toward the cove where we could see the dock, the boat slowed and finally stopped. We backed up and tried again. Three times until the boat was close enough to the dock for the gang-plank to reach, and off we went.

We figured we had one hour to get to the cabin, look around, pack up Mike's things, and get back to the dock to catch the *Norrskär*. So, off through the woods and over the rock, Mike wading through the water and snow in rubber galoshes, and me hopping the puddles with my leather combat-boots. The cabin was being used by someone else who was cutting. A saw, chain, and gasoline tanks were about, and a wet rubber work suit was lying on the bed. The dirty dishes from October stood undisturbed in the wash basin, coagulated grease floating on the water and clinging to the china.

LETTERS

[5 March 1971 letter to Bruce's folks continues]

. . . Here [in Namdo], where I had been trying to reach for three days, it seemed a bad idea to return with Rosemary for Easter vacation. Reality makes such short shrift of our fantasies. We were off again through the woods in less than ten minutes, alternately finding and losing our previous path; back to the dock with ten minutes to spare. Mike went off to find bits of nature to take back to Lisa "or else she'll think I wasn't thinking of her," while I rolled a smoke. We sat on the dock in the sun at noon and ate peanut butter and BLT sandwiches and drank beer and listened to the water melt and the wind blow and laughed as best our full mouths allowed.

The boat came and cut a new channel going out, and we settled into the upper deck smoking room and watched it all drift by, listened to the water and rapped nautical terms. What's the back—stern; what's the width—beam; until we came to trigonometry, celestial navigation, and finally got lost in our heads where we were plotting to go. "Have you got your sea legs?" Mike asked.

About those articles on Sweden that you sent us. They're mostly filled with lies, that is, they reflect the views of the American yellow press and their representatives in Sweden who run around with a segment of Swedish opinion which is not representative of the country. Parker S. is doing a master's thesis on the treatment of American deserters in Sweden (content analysis of two-and-a-half years of coverage by the major Swedish newspapers). Roughly, the American coverage is parallel to that of the most conservative paper here. To understand any country is an object lesson in the relativity of values, as you can well appreciate from your experience in Latin America. Suffice it to say that the American press supports American foreign policy. This becomes increasingly obvious the longer one lives outside of the country. Just as the majority of opinion in the US supports an end to the war, the vast majority of European opinion not only wants an end to the senseless destruction of a peasant country, they are continually amazed at the stupidity and lack of foresight of American leadership. The image of America as the land of the free and the savior of democracy, an image dating from the revolution and most recently reinforced in the Second World War, has been seriously if not permanently eroded. I speak of this image not so much as an abstraction as a reality reflected on the personal and cultural level. Since the capitalists are in charge all over the western world, this cannot be said to apply so much to economics. Those who define value and accumulate wealth work according to their own laws.

On this level, perhaps it is sufficient to say that the imperatives of domestic control of the economy are beginning to be appreciated in this the fourth decade of the American imperia.

It is becoming clearer that the technocratic society most clearly profits those at the center, i.e., communications, electronics, and sophisticated hardware. I understand that Nixon has proposed a crash program to retrain unemployed engineers and technicians on the West Coast (aerospace layoffs). When the social democratic government talks about the people, the correspondence is much more real . . .

[unsigned]

7 April 1971[42]

Once upon a time there was a little boy named "Creeping" and a little girl named "Innocuousness"—or the other way around: it doesn't matter much because the two were, *inter alia*, inseparable friends. One day Creeping and Innocuous went to the movies where they saw a horrifying film called, *The Chemical Men Invade Earth*. In short, the story was this: The Chemical Men, who had tried unsuccessfully to invade Earth several times earlier, were now concentrating all their efforts on a final invasion attempt—Operation Opprobrium! Allied with a rather feeble group of wicked incentives, they faced the united forces of the constraints, which had also been gathering strength for a final bout. During the battle it became clear that the incentive forces had actually been weakened, rather than strengthened, by their recent "incursion" into Southeast Mars. Rather than suffer ignominious defeat, The Chemical Men withdrew to their hidden impenetrable laboratories; the threat therefore remains hanging over the earth: will The Chemical Men

42   This story is attributed to Rosemary.

invade again? Creeping and Innocuousness walked home in a very thoughtful mood. They were afraid of the threat; in fact, they were afraid of the very creeping innocuousness of The Chemical Men. So, they decided, as a first line of defense, to join forces and live together as Odious Taboo.

Chapter Ten
Canadian Road Trip

Bruce, 2008–2009

By the summer of 1971, I wanted out of the rat race of driving taxi, out of the three to noon shift, out of a road to nowhere except more of the same. I thought I could do better in Canada and applied at their embassy to immigrate. The official information suggested that there was a shortage of teachers in Canada and I indicated that that was my chosen career.

I was somewhat disquieted by the Swedish recruitment material, suggesting Canada was looking for diamond drillers, heavy equipment mechanics, miners, and roughnecks to work the oil-fields of Alberta. An exploratory trip seemed in order. Before hearing back from the Canadian embassy on my application, Rosemary and I planned a six-week vacation to Canada and wrote to family to arrange visits with them while there.

Rosemary and I arrived in May at Montreal and took a train to Gananoque, Ontario, located across the St. Lawrence River from upstate New York in the Thousand Islands area. It was a classic small-town railroad station, except it was not in the town but north of it on the mainline, amidst fields and dirt roads. Nobody there. The waiting room was locked as was the stationmaster's office. It seemed no one got off there. We sat on our bags and waited. Brother Alan and his latest girlfriend, Susan, were to meet us at the train station with their car. "They know where to meet us," I said.

"I hope they didn't have trouble," said Rosemary.

"It's only been half an hour. I wonder where the town is." I looked up again at the sign on the station, *GANANOQUE*. "It must be over there somewhere," I pointed south, toward where I knew from the map the St. Lawrence River must be. I turned around, looked north and saw that the land flattened out into fields for several miles. The only access to the station was a gravel road running east and west, and turning again, I saw a car approaching from the west. I held my breath in anticipation, not knowing what kind of car Alan had. No . . . the car never slowed at the station turn-off and quickly disappeared behind the trees to the east, hidden in its own dust.

Another half hour passed, and we saw nobody. A long freight train rumbled through, but it never even slowed down for Gananoque.

By this time, I was thinking about *Waiting for Godot* and my life in particular. Here, at a train station in Canada, under a clear sky on a beautiful day. All that life seemed to be about was waiting for the next thing to happen. Patience and being in the present was the challenge and to enjoy it was the trick. It was getting warm in the afternoon sun and we had moved our luggage into the shade and made ourselves as comfortable as we could on the one outside bench. A car appeared in my line of vision, turned into the station's access road. *This will be them*, I thought. I did not move. I was enjoying a calm and meditative state. I did not hold my breath. Finally, the excitement of seeing my brother again got the better of me as Alan's car crunched to a stop in the parking space at the foot of the stairs leading up to the bench. Rosemary was on her feet and said, "Get up, Bruce."

"We got lost," Alan said as we embraced. Introductions were made. Alan would be married to Susan in two years. Neither he nor Susan had met Rosemary, even though she and I had married in December 1967, four-and-a-half years previously. The four of us set off for the park we had located on the map.

There was just one other family in the entire campsite and they had taken the best site, on a rocky point overlooking the St. Lawrence River upstream. Their tent was there, but no car or people, so we found the next best site, out of view, set up our tents and began to prepare dinner. For that meal, Susan made the first of many cornbread-in-a-coffee-pee-can dishes over the fire.

I said, "What do you mean cornbread-in-a-coffee-pee-can?"

Susan said, "You make cornbread in a coffee can over the fire."

"But, can't you use a clean can . . . why use the pee-can . . . is it sanitary?"

"I rinsed it out; it's going to bake at umpteen degrees and kill everything anyway."

"Oh . . . couldn't we use a different can?"

"Sure, where's the other can?"

I looked around in the gathering darkness . . . another can . . . I saw no other can . . . I had met my match . . . and the cornbread was excellent. Everybody was feeling good and I was happy. There was a bottle of wine to share.

The next day, the family on the point left early and I immediately staked out the site and we moved tents and kit before breakfast. By mid-day, brother Dan and his wife, Judy, arrived in their VW Bug.

Yes, they were good times, all right, and when they weren't good, they were interesting. The campground north of Toronto was private, which is to say not bucolic, just open ground, near the highway and within sight of it, what used to be a pasture, with the outbuildings converted into makeshift shitters with some outside sinks, but no showers. The tents were no further than 10 feet apart on grassless packed dirt. Fortunately, it did not rain.

The denizens of this derelict dustbin were mostly burned-out hippies. The proximity of people made for impromptu introductions as the dazed and unwashed wandered the site.

"Wanna try some acid, man?" or "Woodstock was really far out, were you there?" or, even further out, "I've got Paul Newman's long-distance charge number, he supports us you know, you could use it; I have, we all have, it's OK with him, he said so."

We camped in the Niagara Peninsula to see Niagara Falls on a cloudy day and returned through the rain and high winds. Everybody was thinking the same thing as the rain began but only started talking about it when we were 20 minutes away from our site. Only then could we not deny that the site would be swamped, and the winds might be sufficient to damage the tents.

Dan said, "We have to be prepared—I think I know where the rope is—I have a knife here," patting his pocket; "we'll have to get right on it."

As we pulled into the driveway of the small private campground, we strained to see our site though the murky afternoon light, driving rain, and lightning. We had to pass the owner's house to see the spot where we camped, amid a small copse of trees in the middle of a small field.

"Holy shit . . . look at that," Dan said to the afterimage of a nearby lightning strike.

"What?" I missed the flash's illumination, looked where Dan was looking, but saw nothing but rain and darkness.

"It's a mess," he said.

"Where's the track?" I asked, not wanting the car to get mired in mud on the low spots of the field.

"There it is . . . I've got it." Dan steered the car carefully and slowly along the dirt ruts, some parts already acting like gutters from the runoff.

As the car's headlights fell upon the campsite, Dan's breath left his chest. "Shit," he said again.

We sat in shocked silence, gazing through the windshield and rain, the wipers flopping in quick time—tent sides flapping, caved in from the force of the wind, belongings left outside overturned, the kitchen's fire pit and cooking gear all exposed to the weather, tarpaulin lying on the ground like a sopping, discarded green handkerchief, tethered at only one point where the peg and line had held.

Nobody wanted to move. It was warm and dry in the car.

"Did you roll up the sleeping bags?" Dan asked Judy, seeing that the water was pouring onto their tent's floor from the spinnaker-shaped top fly.

"I don't remember," said Judy.

Rosemary and I, Alan and Susan, all were wondering the same thing and imagining even worse, but we said nothing. We did not want to ask or be asked. Silence seemed the best strategy.

"I have to save my instruments," Alan said.

Susan said, "I put them in the trunk, for safekeeping."

"Wonderful . . . thanks." Alan relaxed a bit.

"Well, here goes," said Dan, opening the car's door and ducking out into and against the driving rain. We five watched as Dan darted about the site and scurried back to the car with the preliminary damage assessment report, back in less than two minutes and not yet soaked through.

"We need to strike the tents, get things under cover," said Dan.

No longer able to avoid the inevitable, Rosemary, Alan, Susan, and I piled out of the car, through the muck, toward the tents in the rain—vulnerable gear was hastily wrapped in ponchos or anything watertight—tents brought down on top to further shield from damage—photos and prize possessions grabbed and stuffed into pockets—and we retreated to the warmth of the car.

"Try not to drag mud into the car," Alan said. "The seats have just been reupholstered." Most of us left shoes in the mud and climbed in with sodden socks. "I'll turn up the heat," said Alan. "We have to get dried out." Sodden and grumpy, we six sulked.

Alan rolled down the lee side window, wrung his socks out. With six people in a car designed for four, the ensuing passing of socks became a mystic exchange of sodden clothing, to be wrung out and passed back, Alan presiding.

We stayed that night in the house of the landlord, gratefully, and used his dryer non-stop, finally falling into a sleep without wind and rain, in his basement.

"Ontari-erio you lovely dog you, when you're not rainin', we're not complainin'," a song by Alan, composed while driving north—of Barrie—north of Lake Huron—pulling off the road at a Provincial, unknown campground—leaves barely in bud—more cornbread-in-a-pee-can. Susan knit me a toque. Frost overnight.

Northern Ontario in mid-May can be cool, especially at night, and particularly when it rained. Alan played the guitar and mandolin and composed songs, one for each of the provinces that were traversed. I found Northern Ontario to be much like the country around Stockholm: pine forests, hilly shield rock and lakes, but fewer people and rawer.

The rawness is in the country—fewer roads, the towns widespread and usually with a single industry—a pulp mill in Dryden, the grain silos, and port at Thunder Bay. The beverage rooms are loud, peopled by mill workers, lumberjacks, and truck drivers. Food and gas are cheap compared to Sweden. Everything is bigger, not just in Ontario but everywhere in Canada—big as in the Niagara Falls, Lake Superior, the Great Plains, the Rocky Mountains, Montreal, Toronto, and Vancouver. The trains are longer, some with over 100 cars. In Sweden a long train is 20 cars. The distances are vast by European standards. As the bird flies, from Montreal to Vancouver is 2,400 miles. If the bird flies the same distance southeast from Stockholm, it won't stop till it reaches Kuwait. Driving to Kuwait would not be recommended, but driving to Vancouver—hey, why not? Let the good times roll.

From Thunder Bay west, Rosemary and I rode with Alan and Susan in their 1960 Ford Falcon—through bogs and lowlands that zigzagged beneath power lines, their long loping curves draped between towers of steel. Up the north side, cross under and west on the south side. This went on for some time. The plan was for Dan's VW and Alan's Falcon to rendezvous in Banff.

"Seems to be a lot of smoke coming out of the exhaust," I said at one point.

"Not a problem," said Alan, "I just had it overhauled."

"Then why do we have to keep adding a quart of oil every three hundred miles?"

"I guess the engine needs it," said Alan.

After meandering through this quagmire, we came upon Aaron Provincial Park, east of Dryden, Ontario, and turned north off the Trans-Canada, down a quarter mile access road to the campsite.

Behold, stretching before us was a fan-shaped campground, on a lake. We quickly found the best site, on the northwest side of a peninsula, looking over the water, toward the late afternoon sun, sparkling on the wave tops into our appreciative and tired eyes. Few others were around—it was still early in the tourist season.

Dan pulled the Beetle's front end close to the fire-pit of our site. I thought—*maybe two hours of daylight left.*

We were all hungry. Dan said, "Let's cook before we set up the tents."

The women brought the food and cooking gear to the campsite's picnic table. We men situated the table to the windward side of the fire pit and rustled up firewood and water from the common spigot. The table was piled high with food and cooking gear; there was no place for Dan to sit. "I have an idea," he said. "We could unload the luggage in the VW's trunk onto the seats inside and use the empty trunk as our kitchen."

Not a bad idea, I thought since the car was already parked right next to the fire pit. From the picnic table, Dan and I brought the box of kitchen utensils, condiments, dry goods (flour, cereal, bread, coffee, oil, margarine), paper plates, dish detergent, and the bucket we used for washing dishes to the trunk of the VW—our new kitchen. Now there was room for everyone at the table.

I sat down to enjoy the fire and have a smoke. By now, the women had peeled potatoes for boiling and prepared the steaks for the grill. The fire had started to form coals.

"We'll get it sorted out," said Dan.

"It should work," I said.

The meal was good and sitting around the fire that night after a gorgeous Canadian sunset, it was too cold for Alan's fingers to play guitar, so we sang camp songs a cappella and turned in early.

I wore my sweater to bed and advised Rosemary to bundle up. We put our jackets over the sleeping bags for extra warmth.

I shuddered out of my bag early the next morning. I needed to pee. On my way to the outhouse, I noticed frost on the cars' windshields. Alan was standing by the fire pit when I returned. Gazing into the ashes, he said, "The women say they won't get up until they have coffee."

We didn't have coffee and I said, "There must be a gas station or store close by—I remember seeing a sign on the highway just before we turned off."

We scraped the frost from the windshield of the Falcon. Alan got in, put the key into the ignition switch and turned it on. It was slow to crank . . . coughed . . . caught to life. Alan put it in drive and headed up toward the bottom of the access road. Just when we got there, ready to go up the hill to the highway, the little red oil light came on.

"Hmmm," said Alan, "That's never happened before."

"Maybe it needs oil," I said.

Alan shut off the engine, popped the hood, got out, and pulled the dipstick. I got out and watched.

"See," said Alan, "plenty of oil—but it sure looks black and thick," showing me the paper towel. "Let's see if we can make it to the gas station—we'll need to be there anyway, if something needs to be done."

Back in the Falcon, Alan drove up the hill—I kept my eye on the little red light. It stayed on. Just as we turned onto the deserted Trans-Canada, the engine began to make deep, guttural sounds.

"I can see the gas station," I said, pointing down the road, just beyond a slight rise in the road.

"If we can make it over the rise," said Alan, "I'll turn off the ignition and we can coast into the station."

But, just as we crested the rise, a deep clanking noise arose from under the hood, Alan reached for the ignition key, a final loud clank arose, and the engine quit.

"Shit," he said.

I got out of the car. "Is it in neutral?" I asked through the open door, "I'll push."

It took the two of us to get the Falcon rolling downhill to the station, where we pulled in, stopped and parked.

The station did not appear open. We cranked the windows and caught our breath after pushing. *What next?* I thought.

We debated whether one of us should hike back to the campsite. Neither of us was willing, so we waited—only 15 minutes till they opened, according to the sign on the door. But the time to open came and went, then Dan showed up in the Beetle.

"What's up?" he asked, and I told the story.

The three of us looked under the engine of the car and found a black pool of oil mixed with water. "This doesn't look good," Dan said.

Within two hours, after the station opened and the mechanic had arrived, put the Falcon on a hoist and dropped the oil pan, the verdict got clearer. The mechanic said, "The oil pump shaft broke— the engine threw a connecting rod that punched a hole in the engine block. You'll need a new engine."

"A new engine," said Alan, "I just had it overhauled."

"At a dealer?" the mechanic asked.

"No—a backyard mechanic," said Alan, crestfallen as he realized the implications of his answer.

The mechanic shook his head.

"How about a used engine?" asked Alan.

"I'll check around," said the mechanic and went to the station's phone.

The verdict got worse. The mechanic reported that there were no used engines among the car graveyards in the vicinity. A rebuilt one could be shipped from Toronto, but it would take at least a week to arrive. With shipping and installation, it would cost more than Alan had paid for the Falcon two years prior.

We retreated to the campsite and prepared a quick lunch. "Six of us can't travel in the Beetle," said Dan. This was the situation, as I saw it: Rosemary and I were totally reliant on my brothers for wheels; we were in the middle of nowhere in Northern Ontario; I was prepared for and expected that Alan and Susan might abort the trek and return by train to upstate New York where they lived; Dan seemed to want to press on west; Rosemary was silent, closely watching the dynamics of the brothers and wives.

When lunch was finished, Dan said he had an idea, but would not discuss it. He wanted to go into Dryden with Alan and Susan to check some things out. By the time they got back to the campsite, much had happened. The three of them had gone down to the railroad station and Alan had bought himself and Susan a day coach ticket straight through to Banff, leaving late that afternoon; they had rounded up some boxes in which to pack their stuff; they had sold the Falcon to the gas station owner; the back of the Beetle was filled with the remaining contents of the Falcon.

Alan and Susan had to pack and make it to the train station for a 4:44 p.m. departure. We galvanized into action. Susan said, "Divvy up the kitchen equipment—we'll have to camp in Banff until you catch up with us there in the Beetle—strike the tent—Alan, we have to sort through the stuff from the Falcon—we're going to have to throw some things away."

"I'll pack some food for the train trip," said Rosemary.

"I'll pack your tent," I said.

"I'll divvy up the kitchen equipment," said Dan.

"I'll pack our clothes and sleeping rolls," said Susan.

We were getting good at breaking camp after a week of shakedown. As the must-leave-now time for the train approached, Alan got stuck on the miscellaneous shit from the Falcon. Having decided to travel in style, he'd brought his guitar, mandolin, lots of tapes for the new player in the Falcon with improved speakers—hard to let go. A big wire trash bin began to fill with maps of upstate New York, damaged tapes, and paperback books. The Falcon's registration certificate went into the fire's embers where it lay for a moment, turned all brown, began to smoke, then popped into flames.

I took Alan and Susan to the Canadian Pacific station in Dryden. They stood next to their boxes, away from the clump of passengers further down the platform. They had been told that this would be where the freight car would stop; they would help load their boxes and then go forward to the passenger cars. For the coach, Alan had the same knapsack he was carrying when he visited me in Stockholm in the summer of 1969 and his guitar in hand. Susan was carrying bags of food, books, and the mandolin.

When the train pulled in and stopped, the boxes were loaded on the freight car, along with someone else's bicycle. As the three of us walked forward toward the coaches, Alan said, "Could you loan me some money, we're broke."

I had some cash; Rosemary had insisted that I cash some traveler's checks that morning. "You mean no money at all?" I asked.

"Nothing," said Alan.

I looked at Susan. She shook her head. I pulled out all of the cash in my wallet and handed it to Alan. "See you in Banff," I said as we embraced. Alan and Susan climbed into the coach, banging guitar and mandolin cases against the railings of the stairs as they negotiated the narrow passage.

When I returned to the campsite, the fire had been fed. I agreed that it would be best to spend the night here and rocket off toward Banff in the morning. I paced the site, picked Alan's paystubs out of the trash bin and threw them on the fire as Dan watched. "Why did you do that?" he asked.

"No use leaving personal evidence. What about the car?" I asked Dan.

"Oh," Dan said, "you mean, was it legal?"

"Yes."

"Well," said Dan, "as you said, you're not supposed to bring a car into Canada and then sell it."

"Right."

"That gas station owner—the guy who bought it—didn't seem to care. He offered Alan $130 and charged him $80 for the diagnostic work—leaving $50 for Alan and that's what the train ticket to Banff cost for him and Susan. They're broke."

"I guess we'll have to back him from here," I said, not really knowing where "here" was except that money would be needed.

I gazed out over the fire to the afternoon sunlight sparkling off the lake to the west and imagined that I was in a warm coach—the rails going clickity-clack, clickity-clack—through cuts blasted out of the shield-rock to level the right of way—through swamps over causeways of granite-fill from the cuts—winding around domes of rock, lichens, and the never-ending pines—through the windows, blankly watching the telegraph wires swoop down and then up again to the punctuation of poles. "We should make supper," Dan said . . .

Alan, 2014

The train ride to Banff was like over-nighting in a moving village. Susan and I traipsed the narrow aisles between cars, slept in two cramped and stacked beds in the sleeper coach, and spent the daylight hours upstairs on the observation deck talking to fellow travelers, reading and watching the Canadian scenery slip by. At one point, a huge black bear loped along side of the train trying to keep up. The Trans-Canadian started in Montreal and went all the way to Vancouver.

With Bruce's cash, we were able to buy food in the dining car and snacks from the porter who roamed up and down the aisles of the passenger car. "Get your T-Bones," he'd say winking at us, "fifty cents." It was rumored that the porter could also get you fixed up with a "date" for the night. But that cost twenty Canadian dollars.

Bruce, 2008–2009

. . . The next morning, the four of us broke camp and hit the road for an early breakfast in Dryden and then west on to Kenora. Dan drove; he said he liked it. I was glad not to drive—I had become used to the idea that driving was something you were paid to do.

So, with Dan driving and Judy, his wife, in the front, it was on to Kenora. The topography changed, from the bogs east of Dryden, to the shield-rock west—then through the twists and turns into Kenora. I looked out the rear window— "Indians," I said, seeing the pedestrians on the street as we snaked through the town.

Rosemary said, "There must be reservations around here."

On to the Manitoba border—across the bogs and sandy flat pine-lands toward Winnipeg—around the city on the south bypass and a quick stop for lunch at the McDonald's on West Portage Avenue and then on to Portage la Prairie—getting dizzy on the way from the flatland—stretching to the horizon—and on through the spirit sands to Brandon, where we stopped for dinner at a café south of the Assiniboine River bridge on 18th Avenue—and then on to Virden, where we found a motel and crashed for the night.

From western Manitoba at Virden, west into Saskatchewan, rolling along, up, down, and over the hills past Regina—through the towns of Moose Jaw and Swift Current—past mountains of sulphur—into the high plains southeast of Calgary, following the Trans-Canada, into oil country.

We missed Alan and his song-making. In Saskatchewan, Dan came up with: "Catch-a-snatch, catch-a-snatch, catch-a-snatch-a-katchewan." I think he was just horny.

The provincial campsite that we had picked from the map seemed perfect; we were at the end of the day, tired and ready to pull over. As we approached the location, I spotted a huge tipi-shaped structure off to the northwest of the highway. Sure enough, there was an exit here, with a campground logo showing the way to get off. We cruised the campground for the best site—there seemed few criteria to choose from—away from the highway noise and close to the toi-let facilities—and so we pitched our tent and only then noticed the sound of oop-sla, oop-sla, with a high creaking metallic whine in the background.

"What is that?" asked Dan.

I listened, "I don't know."

The two of us looked east, across the highway, where the sounds seemed to be coming from. In the failing light of sunset, we were able to make out jack-beams pumping oil—sucking out the life-blood of the post-industrial age—through the twilight and on through the night. We all slept, uninterrupted, to my knowledge, and when the sun rose, I was ready to leave and feeling like my peace of mind had been sucked dry, my mouth like powder, swallowing energy-or-else, as the Beetle scurried on to Calgary and west into the Rocky Mountains.

Approaching the Rocky Mountains from the east, once clear of Calgary, is an awesome sight. Snow-covered ridges—highway up the valley—through the first ridge and on to Banff. We found the camp-site—Alan and Susan were ecstatic.

"Now we can *really* eat—tell me about the trip—look at this view, Bruce—over the valley—down there's the Banff Springs Hotel . . ."

The hotel was a six-story chateau in the Canadian Pacific tra-dition of early century luxury with a hot spring up the valley from there—sweeping panoramas of mountain landscape. Alan, Susan, Dan, and Judy had never seen such mountains—I had hiked in the Sangre de Cristo Mountains of northeast New Mexico in high school and found these to be more majestic, sweeping in their vistas, open to a more turquoise sky.

The kitchen-under-the-bonnet was nosed up to the fire-pit, the kitchen gear reintegrated and supper made with provisions from the VW. Alan and Susan were without and had sung for last night's supper in one of the sheltered fire-pits behind the Tunnel Mountain campground. They had moved into a superb campsite on the brow of the ridge overlooking the valley below. They had somehow hauled their gear up five kilometers of road from the railroad station to the campsite, hauled it by hand, leg over leg—like a portage to higher ground . . .

Alan, 2014

The following is part of a poem that I wrote about our excursion that summer:

> Banff: north slope of Mt. Norquay,
> long johns too hot,
> wishing I were in a jock strap & headband.
> Bruce produces a jaw breaker, "Special
> Sherpa climbing aid," he says with ceremony.
> Layer by layer, cinnamon on the crags
> above the tea house, fruit-punch and licorice
> where the snow drifts stop us
> from reaching the summit.
>
> Inside our tents,
> smoke and hair unfasten.
> The moon commences
> to roll through its dark meaning—
>
> If breath were green,
> the trees would weep still water.
> Dandelions arrange the curve
> of your back into this:
> a train arriving.
> We are the first to step off.

Bruce, 2008–2009

. . . We stayed several nights in Banff, saw the local sights and mountain sheep, but wanted to get on to Vancouver, without room for Alan and Susan in the Beetle who stayed at the campsite.

I had a contact living outside of Vancouver. We found it easily, off a gravel road, a small acreage with no visible neighbors. A couple of hippies greeted us. I did not sleep well there. The property had deep woods to the south and, I was told, the US border was less than a mile away. I had dreams of being abducted. I did not know my hosts. Was this a set-up? It would be easy for a special team to abduct me over the border.

But Vancouver was beautiful. We did the sights: Stanley Park, the Aquarium, Chinatown for dim sum. Then back to Banff where we split up again. Dan and Judy drove back to Ontario.

Alan, Susan, Rosemary, and I took the train. We had coach tickets and it was non-stop to Toronto, much easier to ride than to drive. We spent the day on the top floor of the astrodome coach and watched the prairies and woodlands east of Winnipeg roll by. We finally met up with the rest of the family at Rondeau Provincial Park on Lake Erie. Big reunion. Bob and Ella Mae joined us there as well as Rosemary's brother Eric, sister Carol (who was pregnant with her third child), and her husband, Joe. The road-gang of six dispersed; Rosemary and I toured a bit in Quebec before being dropped at the Montreal airport for the flight back to Stockholm. My father asked before we left, "Is there anything you need or want that you can't get in Sweden?"

Knowing that they had already given me almost everything that was important in life, I answered, "Reese's Peanut Butter Cups." He took me straight to a grocery store and bought me a family pack of 48.

The 1971 family reunion at Rondeau Provincial Park, Ontario, Canada.
Back row, left to right: Dan, his wife, Judy, Rosemary, Bruce (mugging for the
camera with a salacious grin—note his forefinger poking through the zipper in his
trousers), Father Bob, and Bruce's brother-in-law, Joe Kozlevcar.
Seated on the far side of the table, left to right: Alan and his girlfriend, Susan.
Seated on the near side of the table, left to right: Mother Ella Mae and Carol
Kozlevcar holding her children, Mark and Joey.
Eric, Rosemary's brother, is taking the picture.

Chapter Eleven
"I Must Get Out of Here"

LETTERS

July 1971

Dear Family,

On the trip back to Sweden from Canada, we each had three seats across, so the plane was not too bad. I slept through dinner, but Rosemary ate and said later she wished she hadn't. Copenhagen in the morning, airport crowded, bought cheese, and flew north. Finally got home 14:30 local time and wandered around in a daze, which is only now beginning to disappear. Rosemary went back to work the next day, and I got this job here straightened out. It looks like we will be here during the week and in Solna on the weekends, so you all can write to either address. Sweden is more deadly boring than expected and the weather here reminds us of the first week on the Niagara Peninsula. Almost all of the pictures did not come out due to . . . pilot error? (somebody else's camera) time warp key-hole saw teeth cuts marring plywood to ribs for kayak

worked all day, wash stairs, three each, three flights
and the stoop
like some old colored woman in Baltimore on Saturday
      morning
gray sky and water in the gutter

ancient sea animal skeleton in the stone
guts tied up too much cheese
the black freighter . . .

[Unsigned]

Toward the end of August 1971

Dear Family,

Wherever this may find you, in East Hampton, or else-where, in a state of no-mind or no-nonsense, riding the waves of karma, feeling perhaps strange thoughts, reflections. That is all I can send you . . .

We have moved . . . we can now both walk to work. I drove six days this week and today is Sunday. Off to the Modern Museum to see an exhibition on modern utopia. The last good week of weather is slipping away under an advancing low. Next week is big plans for Yugoslavia.

Seem to have wandered into a state of clarity.

[Unsigned]

Bruce, 2008–2009

After Canada, the routine of taxi began to pale. I thought a better alternative was Canada. However, shortly after my return to Stockholm, the Canadian Embassy informed me that my application had been denied; there was no shortage of teachers and they did not need me. And so began the 1971/1972 year.

I started working on a casual basis for a taxi owner who had a fleet of dozens of cars. They always seemed glad to have drivers. But I had an accident (in the spring of 1972), and had to explain this to officials at Taxi Central. I was in one of those traffic circulars, and the guy in front of me had pushed his right of way on the yield. I flowed in behind him, and then the guy, for no reason, hit his brakes and stopped. I was right behind and thought, *what an asshole*, to come to a dead stop for no visible reason. I managed to stop just short of his rear bumper and then thought, *fuck you mother*, accelerated, and ran into him.

Jumping out of my taxi, I said, "Gee, I'm sorry," admitting my fault; after all, I had rear-ended him. After that, I knew my taxi-driving days were numbered. I drove less often; the authorities said nothing. I thought more often about Canada.

I was also drinking more. On my days off, I would meet up with Dave G., buy a bottle of scotch, and ride the bus or the subway to the end of the line. When on the upper level of the London-type bus, in the middle of the day, we would sit in the front and drink scotch. I had never been a heavy drinker, but was becoming one, and I didn't like it.

I must get out of here, I thought.

Already, some of the guys in the Network had decided the same and gone back to the ol' United States. Most were getting four months in the brig and a dishonorable discharge. Then a senator stood up and said, "Yes, I too, was a deserter—I was wounded in the Italian Campaign, driving north against the Nazis—I was wounded and sent to the rear hospital—they said that I needed to recuperate—but my buddies were catching it from the Huns—so, yes, I deserted, against orders, from the hospital and made my way north to my unit—and rejoined them—to fight the enemy out of Italy."

Back to the present: Shortly, there were reports that guys were getting four years—they were on the planes going back—they thought they'd be in for four months—so much for politics. The senator I quoted previously was Daniel Inouye from Hawaii; he was Japanese and knew that shit abounded when enemies were at your gate. Plead loyalty in these times of trouble.

I found the Swedes had different attitudes toward alcohol than the United States. First, I noticed that in the United States the rule seemed to be "hold your alcohol," that is, drink, but don't show it. In Sweden, the rule seemed to be "drink and show it," like it was a release from the usual constraints; everybody knew you acted differently and expected no less.

I attended parties, many of them in nice big apartments. I remembered one where there were 12–15 people, mostly couples, up to middle age, solid middle class. Within two hours, several people were talking to Ralph on the big white telephone (barfing into the toilet). Arguments would break out among couples—the issue: who would drive home. If unresolved, they would call a taxi and come back the next morning by subway and retrieve their car. You definitely did not drink and drive. Some foreign tourists learned how strict things were when they spent 90 days in jail after being arrested under the influence in a rented car.

Old men (*gammal gubbe*) would stager around the subway cars brandishing a bottle of vodka in a paper bag on weekend evenings. Binge drinking seemed normal then. The liquor stores closed early and could only be found on side streets with no neon lights—the picture of drabness. Shoppers brought in their briefcases so that nobody would know they were carrying liquor—what will the doorman or the neighbors say?

There was prohibition until the mid-fifties. Alcohol and particularly vodka tends to be endemic in Russia, Finland, Sweden, and Iceland. The Danes drink beer and the Norwegians keep it a secret—the "Vodka belt." In Sweden alcohol is heavily taxed—a very expensive habit. In Iceland you could only buy yeast at the liquor store—why was yeast a controlled commodity?—of course, because you could distill whatever with it.

Other parties were more sober, featuring food—like a huge mound of seafood pilaf. And at one party, I arrived before the other guests to help prepare the food. I learned that the guest of honor was the political leader of the Angolan front for national unity—or was it some other country? It really didn't matter—the people were oppressed, the existing government backed by the United States, suppression the rule, under the guise of law—help the good guys (and this guy could be the next prime minister). In an apartment overlooking a tidy suburb of Stockholm, the politico's security arrived first, conferred with the hostess about all the guests, and only then, amid a shuffle of welcome and beneficent gestures, in the Swedish tradition, he was introduced to each guest.

I was a war resistor and against US involvement in foreign civil conflicts.

"OK," was the reading on the black man's face—common enemies among the oppressed.

There were other parties, featuring the leaders of other African governments in exile—I got several invitations—I seemed to be playing the role of the official opposition to the United States. I found it tiring—and worse, I was no longer flattered by the role, more put upon me than personally taken. I refused invitations—Rosemary was disappointed—she liked the parties, meeting others, discussing injustice, a mover in her time.

I was thinking, *where can I retire into anonymity—to simply enjoy whatever life brings,* like the Gypsies in *The Seventh Seal,* to dodge evil—to refuse to acknowledge its power—to live in innocence, among the flowers in the sun on a warm day—to drink wine and make love.

And then there were the Swedes. There was a mythology among the underground Americans that the Swedes were boring, deadsville in the head, non-spontaneous—they can't talk to you until you've been introduced—the whole "you" and "thou" of the language (the informal and the formal), the hypocrisy of alcohol, the basic stand-offishness . . . not like Southern California. I thought, *if you're looking for Southern California in Sweden, you are seriously misled. If you miss it so much, then go back.* And, in increasing numbers, they did, to be court martialed or face civil action related to their draft status—often to beat the charges.

Stockholm was being depopulated of American resisters—Bruce B. had gone back to Canada, Dave G. had left for nursing school on the West Coast. The focus was now elsewhere than Sweden—shifting to home side, to the hearts and minds of Americans—the final battleground.

LETTERS

8 December 1971

Dear Alan,

. . . It was the previous week we had the snow; on Tuesday of that week, I was in full acceleration out of a left-turn lane (where I had been waiting the red, first in line), going into the turn, the road contour shifts, slush everywhere, I see a truck on the parabola of my turn, against the curb, stopped. I hit the brakes, and everything locks and starts to breach, so I decide to free-wheel it around the end of the truck and in the process, right fender, hood, and bumper are pushed in on my 1971 Volvo automatic sedan taxi. I pull over, jump out, and inspect the truck damage. Might as well have hit him with a broom for all the damage it did to him. The truck guy got a crowbar and we bent the fender to free the wheel, and I noticed that my right-front tire had very little tread; it just couldn't grab that slush when I free-wheeled it.

Saturday night we went eating and drinking with an English couple, friends from SIPRI. He is an English biological and chemical warfare expert and economic researcher, etc. He laid a copy of *Guerilla Handbook* on me. A Guyanese folk singer laid out some good calypso. "The closer you get to your work, the uglier you become." Proctor, 1971.

Just read *The Day of the Dolphin*, *Pebble in the Sky*, *The Book of Tea*, *The Heart of Buddhist Meditation*, and carry Patanjali with me in the hack.

Love, Bruce & Rosemary

8 December 1971

Dear Folks,

Feels like I owe you a letter. Rosemary filled you in on Thanksgiving and other celebrations. The Swedes are concerned about India/Pakistan and showing their neutral colors. War! Let's see now, repatriation, religion, economic advantage—all have been used to justify it. The new trend is ominous: refugees in sizeable quantities (9 million from East Pakistan, hundreds of thousands from Palestine, millions of Ibos, etc.) are a sticky problem because they are so real, so unlike the extension of super-ego and the fantasies of glory often used before in war. And refugees usually flee into areas where the Malthusian dilemma is so close to being the best characterization of the area. *Det är inte meningen att folk skulle kampa mot varandra*; it's not intended that people should fight each other, say the Swedes and reveal their faith in community and pay the price of control: highest tax burden in the world.

Parker S. recently passed his orals to get his master's and is now trying to figure out how he can drive a cab. The government is actively discouraging the academic life; too many overtrained people and resources disappearing into services . . .

I may be leaving for Canada in May, with Rosemary following after. First, I must see about the possibility of getting landed status and perhaps choose a place to settle before Rosemary would feel secure enough to join me. We just got money back on taxes and are considering a trip. Like most of our adventures, next could be a postcard from . . . ? Thanks for the records, sentimental and true.

I seem to have my skin problem licked. I've substituted apple cider vinegar for salicylic acid in alcohol as a prewash on my hair, then the Tegrin shampoo every three days. Tegrin soap for my face twice a day, baby soap the body, vinegar rough feet, six yeast tablets a day and vitamins plus orange juice. And a good oil on the face after washing. Funny how we are victimized by our male chauvinism; I should have learned all that when I was thirteen . . .

Love, Bruce

19 January 1972

Dear Folks,

There's so much to thank you for . . . The Fritos and bean dip are almost gone. Karin and Paul are finishing it off in the next room; last night had limas and brownies. Grits for breakfast with grape jelly. Too bad it costs so much to send! . . . Rosemary and I went up to Dalarna around Lake Siljan with Karin, Paul, Mary, and Julian for the first week of January, roughed it in a little cottage with wood stove and fireplace—no heat, no electricity. We kept busy cooking, making fires, chopping wood, refilling kerosene heaters and lamps, ice skating, reading, drinking, and playing lots of games (Yahtzee, Scrabble, and cards). I got healthy, Rosemary got a cold, slipped on the ice, and cracked a bone in her left arm, now in a cast, and I've been doing all the cooking, cleaning up, etc., since. For awhile I had to wash her hair and help her shower, put on her clothes, etc. It only hurts when she tries too much, but she doesn't like the cast. We had hoped for snow, but there was no skiing, only ice skating. The whole lake was frozen; we even did some driving around on it; triple spins . . . close to zero traction and no rudder! Back to work this week. Rosemary is left-handed, so she works on manuscripts with a tape recorder, big rush on the year-book. The taxi is as ever, crumpled another fender Thursday the 13th, a lucky day! . . .

The story behind the carving I sent you: when I was working as a janitor this summer at the Jewish-Christian state church and building my kayak, one day I got messed up on the boat and started picking around in one of the store-rooms in the cellar. I found this crucifix which was broken at the intersection of the cross. The base and cross were very rectilinear and insulted what was left, which you've got; so, I decided the spirit needed resurrecting and it couldn't wait until Easter! I'm sure he understands theft and likes the light better than that old cellar . . .

Love, Bruce

Chapter Twelve
Status: Landed

Bruce, 2008-2009

To go to Siljansnäs, we rented a VW Beetle with studded tires. We drove out onto the ice in the bay, open water beyond. The spins were great; get up to 70 kmph, then turn hard right (or left), it starts to slide, lay it over more, whips around (don't get too close to the open water), gun the throttle, whoopee, 360 degrees.

I laid plans to go back to Canada, to go and see what lay there—not as a tourist, but with the intent of staying.

A farewell party was organized for me. The sundry crew met at a public picnic site on the east of the city. It was early in 1972, the snow barely off the roads—but room to pull off and park vehicles. The party was more like a wake—some had brought mickeys, others toke-pipes—and always the wineskins—the women had brought salads, hotdogs, and buns. The parting was sad, but somehow inevitable. There was an undercurrent message I felt aimed at my heart: "So, go and leave us here to deal with the Swedes—and ourselves—without you." Some of my friends who stayed in the United States and fought the fight against the war after 1968 had felt the same thing about me. "We needed you—we missed you—it was a lonely fight without your support." It was as if I was deserting *them*. But I always thought that it was the only thing I could do at the time—participation in the insanity, living underground, or flight to asylum. Off to Canada seemed more of a change in focus than an abandonment of *compadres* and country.

I had tried hard to become a Swede. Although most Swedes were wonderful people, and some beyond any expectation of friendly, Sweden is for Swedes and immigrants tend to face the difficulties that are familiar to all displaced people: alienation; lack of acceptance; language, social, and sometimes religious barriers; and the bottom line is always less than for the original inhabitants (except in the Western Hemisphere).

I went through customs in Montreal and caught a connecting flight to Toronto where brother Dan delivered an aging VW Beetle, a gift from my father. The resister community in Toronto was more into political action than settlement assistance and I was advised to go to Winnipeg where the assistance with getting landed immigrant status was more the focus. So, with the address of the assistance center in Winnipeg in my pocket, I drove there in the spring of 1972, over the same roads taken the previous spring, only this time alone and staying in motels—one in Sault Ste. Marie and the YMCA in Thunder Bay. My dad had delivered the VW from Oklahoma to Dan in upstate New York. It had a good engine and I made good time, arriving in Winnipeg late on an April afternoon, seeing the counselor at the center, in a church basement on Colony Street and Broadway Avenue. The counselor listened and asked, "Do you need a place to stay tonight?"

"Yes."

"We have some names of people who are willing to help."

I nodded.

He shuffled through some three-by-five-inch cards—found one, dialed the number, got a live person on the line, and explained about me. "Yes . . . then tonight is OK?" he said, looking at me, and I nodded. The counselor said, "OK, he'll be right over," and hung up. "Go to this address," and he gave me directions.

I was feeling fortunate indeed—within a half hour I was at a two-story house in Riverbend and she was greeting me at the door—a handsome young woman with two small children. She showed me to a private room—over the east-side porch on the second floor. She asked if I was hungry. I slept well.

LETTERS

Winnipeg, 12 April 1972

Dear Rosemary,

. . . Wish I could say something inspiring, but three-day drive here a drag; got bad chest cold; four feet of snow in Northern Ontario, the same far-out landscape, rocks, and trees, the biosphere stretched thin; uranium, nickel, and lumber food for survival; 40 degrees below zero recently in Winnipeg, damp, cloudy, and depressing. Motley of folk: German, Ukrainian, Indian, French; 31 million bushels of wheat out of the black chernozem; 40 miles to the bush, aspen breakers, marsh and sink, ice-cold sturgeon water, flat-bottomed washout plain, briar breaks and waterfowl flyway south; sheet-ice breaking up, NW wind 15 mph.

Stony and Brenda my spirit protectors, ex-acid freaks from Illinois, sheltered here in a big house, working-woman, two-kids–fronting operation, domestic manpower immigration national tie-in.

Paperwork a drag, eats time's essence; I miss Rosemary. And fireflies. By now Mom and Dad are in Germany.

Dan, Judy, and I saw *A Clockwork Orange* in Toronto. Judy freaked: they're really doing it already (preconditioning). A tremendous play on audience tastes and spoof on psychological process. Media: I wonder what a serious study of the economics of media would turn up? The tuned-in culture, no doubt. Sitting, reflecting, admitting what you know, accepting what you see. Sipping tea, listening to country music, and missing you.

As ever, Bruce

22 April 1972
Winnipeg, Canada

Dear Alan and Susan,

. . . Tomorrow I go down to make an appointment with immigration; after that some waiting before the appointment when I learn whether I'm landed. Must work to justify the abstractions (third order) of bureaucrats! Otherwise, not much new to say. Filling out forms is making me dizzy: listing 28 residences for the past ten years. Good thing summer is coming.

Hail the fertile earth and may we finally match our desires on hill and plain and other stuff in that vein.

Love, Bruce

Bruce, 2008-2009

I went back to see the counselor at the settlement center the next day. He reviewed my papers and listened to my story.

"You have an unusual academic background," the counselor said, "all of this international relations and Latin American area studies—I'm wondering who might be best able to assess this." He leaned back and said, "I'll try to arrange an appointment for you to talk to Lloyd Axworthy. He's the director of the Institute of Urban Studies at the University of Winnipeg. He might be able to help you."

In the meantime, I explored Winnipeg, starting from Riverbend, east to the Red River, and found the phenomenon of river breakup. As in Sweden, river breakup is something that happens to northern rivers and lakes in the spring. In Winnipeg, in 1972, I sat on the bank and watched the river flowing north—to Lake Winnipeg—north then through Norway House and out through Split Lake and the Nelson River on to Hudson Bay, after having broiled through multiple hydro-generating stations to create electricity for Winnipeg, Minneapolis–St. Paul, and points south. Strangely, Ontario Hydro and points west were not considered in the grid.

I went to see Lloyd, and much to my amazement, I was offered a job—with the Institute. "But," I said, "I can't accept payment, which would be working illegally."

"If you want to work, fine," said Lloyd and so I did, without pay while immigration matters still had to be sorted out. "Call this number—ask for an interview for internal application for landed immigrant status."

By the time of the appointment with Immigration, Rosemary had arrived from Sweden and we both went. "They treated me like your appendage," she said, "the focus was on you—how about me?"

I thought that a very good question, but . . . this was 1972, this was Canada, and maybe they had some things to learn that the Swedes had learned in the 1930s. Anyway, the point was to get landed, so that we would be legal, so we could work.

"Fine," said Rosemary, but I knew that it was not fine. Fine was yet to be determined. I dove into work at the Institute—to be working in English—and the inner-city environment of Winnipeg in the early 1970s, a plethora of federal grants to fight the Canadian war on poverty—which could be waged, because Pierre Elliot Trudeau was not cooperating in Vietnam. In fact, hundreds of thousands of American resistors were already in Canada by the summer of 1972—and they were allowed to apply internally, along with everybody else, for landed immigrant status. And so it was that I was landed and began to be paid by the Institute. Applying for landed status internally was closed off as an option in September 1972. *Whew*, I thought, *just under the wire.*

Landed in Canada, able to do whatever, but I could not vote. I was not a citizen. At least I could get paid by the Institute—as it turned out, 50% more than driving taxi in Stockholm, with fewer taxes.

Rosemary and I stayed in Riverbend. We met friends—Kim (to become Malcomson/Barber) who lent us her apartment on Nassau Street, near the heart of the Osborne district.

Paul, Kim's boyfriend said, "But why would you support a political party that advocated gains to be made by a society appropriated by the bourgeoisie?"

Such a good question, I thought, thinking of Trudeau and the Liberals, and Lloyd, my benefactor.

But Winnipeg is a different story.

The short story is, I worked for the Institute for a year and was recruited by the provincial department of Health and Community Services. I worked for the provincial government for 31 years and am retired now. I separated from Rosemary in 1976, when our daughter, Allison, was three years old, remarried in 1986 to Lorna Leader, when we adopted Elise, newly born. I have two grandchildren through Allison and her husband, Andrew Norrie.

The long story may never be told.

April 5, 2011

To Bruce!
Thanks for this
letter; & I'm glad
to hear from you.
Best Wishes,
Jimmy C.

164 Old Mill Road
Winnipeg, Manitoba
Canada R3J3G9

Jimmy Carter
The Carter Center
One Copenhill
453 Freedom Parkway
Atlanta, GA 30307

Dear President Carter;

Thank you for your pardon of Vietnam era military war resisters. I was one of them. I count myself among your fans.

Your decision allowed me to reunite with my family and my country, although I continue to live in Canada.

I am thanking you now before it is too late for either of us. I missed the opportunity to thank Olof Palme for my Swedish asylum from 1968 – 72 and Pierre Trudeau for the same in Canada since 1972.

I am working on my memoirs and letters of my experiences while in Sweden, including my motivations and conflicting loyalties over duty and loyalty during those difficult times.

Sincerely,

Bruce Proctor

Letter of appreciation to former President Jimmy Carter,
including President Carter's handwritten note.

Alan, 2014

In September of 1974, Bruce's mother, Ella Mae, wrote to President Ford urging him to consider pardoning all the war resisters including Bruce. Following are portions of her letter:

> . . . As you have given pardon to a man[43] who held our highest office and betrayed his oath of office and the American people, I pray that unconditional amnesty may now be granted to those of our exiled boys who "searched their consciences" and either betrayed an oath by desertion or went into exile to avoid taking an oath to serve in an undeclared war and, what many believe, an unjust and immoral war in Vietnam. Many of them, I believe, served their country by their defiance and refusal to take part in its mistakes. For them, the desertion and draft evasion often took great courage. Like the men in the White House, they knew what they were doing, but they had no White House protection and could only hope for amnesty after many years of exile.
>
> Conscience, courage, pardon, and amnesty are words which a Christian nation can understand, and the results of which other nations may praise or blame, but which this nation may use to add strength to its system and its national character. Equal justice under the law seems quite impossible for all, but mercy and forgiveness can come from the heart of a nation . . .

In April of 2011, Bruce wrote a letter to former President Jimmy Carter thanking him for upgrading his dishonorable discharge. This new status which Carter granted to selected war deserters on January 21, 1977—his second day in office—allowed Bruce to visit his family and return to the favorite haunt of his youth: East Hampton's Three Mile Harbor.

Bruce died in June of 2011 after a nine-month, in-hospital battle with an undiagnosed gastrointestinal disease. Following several

---

43 Former President Richard Nixon

unsuccessful surgeries, and months of bedridden torment, pain, and tube-feeding, he asked his doctors to send him home.

"You will die if we send you home," they said.

"I know," he said.

Bruce called me a month or so before passing to ask for my support in his decision to leave the hospital and return home to Winnipeg to die. He asked me to send him a poster of Buddha which he tacked onto his hospital wall. He left the hospital and arrived home on a Thursday to a passel of friends and family assembled. On Friday, he was sitting on his patio enjoying the view of the stream that meandered just beyond his backyard fence. When I called on Saturday, he was sipping single-malt scotch with buddies. On Sunday he could barely speak. On Monday, his daughter Allison called me at work. "He's gone," she said. I wrote this poem in his memory:

SOLILOQUY
(For Bruce S. Proctor, 1943–2011)

If heaven loved not the wine,
A Wine Star would not be in heaven . . .
—*"Vindication"* by Li Po, Eighth Century, CE Chinese poet
Li Po, like my brother, Bruce,
died drunk trying to embrace
the moon's reflection on a northern river.
Their eyes filled up and sank.

They both preferred starlight
to straight answers, chased maple seeds
through mind fields,
yet empires sought their counsel.
They were the Tao's tricksters,

greenhouse soldiers,
red-eyed gazers mastering the cloud's
soliloquy. Bruce had a fondness
for single malt, chose to die at home

where each of his final five days
was worth more than months
of hospital abstinence, feeding tubes
and opiate thugs. He hoped
we understood the exquisite value
of home-sipped scotch. Spring again.

Whirling maple seeds rain upon me.
My eyes fill up and sink.

Published (with slight variations) in *Kansas City Voices*

Seven months before he became terminally ill, Bruce sent me his own ekphrastic poem called, "Sushi." Ekphractic poetry comments on or contemplates another art form—in this case a photo of white pelicans eating fish from a Red River spillway. Bruce's poetic sentiment is so like his youthful self: practical, philosophical, mystical, and humorous:

Sushi

Do you fish to live, or live to fish?
    Either way, make it efficient.
    Some say a seine net's best,
But it takes a boat.
Hey, how about hip waders and a hand-held net?
    But you still have to clean and cook them.
    If you want to eat them raw and un-cleaned,
    You might die from the spines going down.
    If you want a truly efficient way,
    Do like these guys.
But you'll have to become a Buddhist,
Otherwise, no hope of reincarnation.
Plus,
    You can soar along ridges,
        Do wing-overs inside thermals,
        Gain height for cross-country,
        Glide to the next lake, stream or pond, or
        Sit in a cove in the sun to digest.

"Red River Pelicans," photo by Phil Hossack, *Winnipeg Free Press*, January 4, 2010.

Used with permission. Bruce based his poem "Sushi" on this photo.

About the Compiler

ALAN ROBERT PROCTOR has published fiction, essays, humor, and poetry in literary journals such as *New Letters, The Laurel Review, Chatauqua, I-70 Review, Hanging Loose, Loon, Crosstimbers, The Rockhurst Review*, and *The Poeming Pidgeon*. He was twice a *Writer's Digest* national poetry finalist, a finalist in the Mississippi Valley Poetry Contest, and a winner in the 2012 *Rex Rogers Formal Poetry Contest* (Whispering Prairie Press). *The Sweden File: Memoir of an American Expatriate* was first published in 2015 and received a featured review in *Kirkus Reviews*. It was also selected as a 2015 "literary star" by the *Kansas City Star* newspaper. Mr. Proctor is delighted to have Open Books Press re-release the memoir. *Adirondack Summer, 1969*, his debut novel, was published by Westphalia Press in the summer of 2018. Mr. Proctor lives in Kansas City, Missouri, with his wife, Dr. Susan Proctor, and their cat, Beans.

About the Author

BRUCE STEVENS PROCTOR received a bachelor's degree from American University in international relations in 1965, and soon after graduation joined the Defense Intelligence Agency (DIA) where he worked with colleagues in the Pentagon. In 1968 he joined the Air National Guard and pursued a PhD but left the United States and moved to Stockholm as a war resister. After four years in Sweden, he immigrated to Canada in 1972. As a new Canadian in Winnipeg, he involved himself in community organizing, and then joined the public service. Bruce was a thirty-year veteran of the Manitoba Department of Advanced Education, managing Aboriginal access to post-secondary education, and was one of several Under Secretaries of Education. He died at his home in Winnipeg surrounded by family and friends in 2011.

CPSIA information can be obtained
at www.ICGtesting.com
Printed in the USA
FSHW010204270719
60409FS

9 781941 799697